HARVEST

Contemporary Mormon Poems

HARVEST

Contemporary Mormon Poems

Edited By

EUGENE ENGLAND

and

DENNIS CLARK

1989
Signature Books   Salt Lake City

96   95   94   93   92   91   90   89   6   5   4   3   2   1

Library of Congress Cataloging-in-Publication Data

Harvest : contemporary Mormon poems / edited by Eugene England and
Dennis Clark.
    p.   cm.
Bibliography: p.
Includes index.
ISBN 0-941214-80-X
    1. American poetry — Mormon authors.   2. American poetry — 20th
century.   3. Mormon Church — Poetry.   4. Mormons — Poetry.
I. England, Eugene.   II. Clark, Dennis, 1945-
PS591.M6H37   1989
811'.508092283 — dc20   89-33854
                                                                      CIP

Book design: Connie Disney

COVER ILLUSTRATION:
LORD OF THE HARVEST, GARY E. SMITH
OIL ON CANVAS

Preface

As editors, we have divided the poets represented in this anthology into those born before 1940 and those born after 1939. Of the two of us, Eugene England (born 1933) selected the poems from the earlier group, those whose authors are fifty or older and who established the new tradition of Mormon poetry described in his commentary. Dennis Clark (born 1945) selected works from the younger poets. As the initial selection was made, we reviewed each other's choices to arrive at the final determination. We chose poems based on our judgment of their quality but tried to make allowance in that judgment for the variety of achievement in the poets. The works of fifty-three poets are included in this collection. They are arranged by the author's year of birth, oldest first, with birth dates ranging from 1901 to 1965. Readers wishing to study the poems in chronological order will find the dates of first publication for most of the poems in the section "Notes on Poets, and Acknowledgements." Poems not listed there by title are published here for the first time.

Two other sections have been added to this collection. The first, "Hymns and Songs," shows some of the contemporary skill and diversity in the kind of verse that represents the earliest Mormon poetic impulse. The second, "Friends and Relations," offers examples of poetry about Mormon country and the Mormon experience by noted poets who have lived among us. It provides some standards for comparison, but more importantly it honors first-rate poets who stand in various kinds of friendship and relationship to the poems in this new tradition.

The bibliographies at the end provide sources and publication histories for the poems included here and a sampling of other titles by each poet which, for reasons of space, we could not include. They also contain a good selection of important secondary sources and special issues of journals focusing on poetry.

One of the worst sins in art is committed by those who edit anthologies in order to publish their own work. But we believe that the best poetry anthologies are produced by poets themselves. Since both of us have been involved, as editors and writers, in the new tradition and its new directions sampled here, we decided to include our own work. Each of us made the selection of the other's poems.

Like most editors and anthologists, we have enjoyed enthusiastic help, encouragement, advice, and suggestions from poets and readers. We thank Robert A. Rees for getting the project going; Lorie Winder Stromberg, Susan Howe, and Elizabeth Shaw Smith for compiling lists of poets, photocopying poems from many magazines, soliciting submissions, and in general reaping the grain; and Barbara L. Carlson and Jill Thompson for data entry and handling final correspondence. The work is very much theirs; the faults remain our own.

Contents

Contemporary Mormon Poems

Friends and Relations

Editors' Commentary

Contemporary
Mormon
Poetry

HELEN CANDLAND STARK

An Early Frost

This year I cannot bear an early frost.
Despoiled of stores, a tardy bee still drains
The emptied cups of broken flowers. The raspberries,
Small, shrunken ghosts, suck amber wine from suns
No longer red. Late-planted squash and frail
Green beans on rocky soil need but a week
Or so to make their destiny.

Life has its cycle and the growing ends — ends
And is put away beyond all caring.
But these small marginal things, they, too, have striven.
Pruned back too early or perhaps too late,
Trampled by beasts, denied a proper shade,
Coming to flower in a searing drought —
Nonetheless, have they not tried to seed?

An apple tree riddled by beetles thrusts
New flowers into summer's heat. Corn beaten
Down stands up again. The torn bark heals.
But this! Against this frost what possible
Defense? The sun goes down and into each
Bright leaf there creeps a poisonous sap, shredding
The silken web of cell, strangling life.
Against this what defense? One cannot yield
Nor fight. Here, then, it comes, the bitter end
To fruiting — blighting the growing tip, slipping
Along the veins, fingering the heart. And then
The sun shines warm upon the blackened stalk!

And yet, and yet — it is the maimed who bloom
Too late. Better the lagging bee, now crystal-
Eyed fall to the grass; better the tarnished
Pollen sift in the tortured ovary cup!
Better all dead in Indian summer after
An early frost. This year, I cannot bear
An early frost.

Marriage Portion

Across resisting waters our Norse sires
Exhorted struggling settlers to apply
Force. Their legendary funeral pyres,
Crimson and dark against a hostile sky,
Stand stark against the years that followed after,
A monument to strain. As heritage we
Have the drive of effort. The heavy rafter
And the perverse steel must yield to urgency.
Utmost endeavor only can oppose
The parching earth. You muscle down defeat.
By labor deserts blossom as the rose;
Weariness choked off yields shining wheat.

So came we to marriage, bent to wrest
From it tranquility, to shape its good
By resolution — only to find a best
That is of other kind, as of a wood,
Sweet with the peace of pause or linnet's trill,
Or one of our hushed mountain peaks above
The checkered fields at home, serene and still.
So in repose we learned to find our love.

Roses from deserts are a brilliant yield
If we prize, too, the lilies of the field.

Winds
(World War II)

"The door shut by itself," my frightened child
Cried in the night. And I, murmuring comfort,
"It is the wind," felt on my face that wind
Which brooks no stopping, shutting and shutting doors
Across the world—

> Granary doors before hungry hands;
> Wood and oil from the cold;
> Ghetto doors where no lintel stained
> For the Chosen God can make bold
> The heart. Itself must drip the stain.
> Doors of churches black in the rain,
> The altar bombed and the stair;
> And the deep dark doors of the seven seas
> And the ships that enter there.

"The door shut by itself," my little child
Wept in the night. And I muted his fears.
But then, alone, I heard the winds of hate
Shriek through the world. Babes in the dark are we,
Longing to hear the One who mastered winds, say
"Peace, peace, be still."

VENETA LEATHAM NIELSEN

Nursery Rhyme

Written on the death of Carl Gustav Jung

Hush a-lorn, newly born
    rose of my love
Into a cabbage patch
    dropped from above

Hush a-wild, tender child
    bone of my grief
Here's a bough broken
    without any leaf

Hush a-lost, tempest tossed
    blood of my pain
Cradle suspended
    on lightning and rain

Hush a-lie, kitten-eye
    dark little mole
Here's a half-burrow
    that ends in a whole

You'll not need a father
    until you've got a soul

Safe may your cradle
    rock in the sun
Hush a-lull breast of gull
    soft little one

My Father Tamed Wild Horses

My father who is eighty shot white bears
In my small Arctic. Crystal igloos
Mounded wastes of boundless snow. He fished
In sawtooth oceans for my frigid food, and flame
That made blue glaciers tumble milk,
Braided gold ears on each cold stalk,
Charmed ruby rings from chunks of chalk,
Prismed the air to sun-sprayed silk. . . .
He gave me dogs, some bones to shape,
A knife, a skin, a game.

My father from magenta dunes could see
Our desert spin, with windrift sand
As hot as comets' tails, and he would spell
The unfixed whirligig to stop, then stitch
Our ragged tent upon a calm;
Would gather dates from mirage palm,
Genie a well of scorpion balm,
Could sing a psalm. . . .
His gateways to our camel's eye
Unnerved the needles of the rich.

My father made an ark so tough
A dove could find it in the sleet
If seas of tempest battered down
Mountains and cliffs, a channel ditch
Where roily waters had to move
Along a stern but seemly groove,
Although the restless current prove
As angular as bitter love. . . .
He gave me for my earliest home
A willow basket caulked with pitch.

My father tamed wild horses down
A fire of jungle vines. Too temperate
For crocodiles, he caged a zoo
Of leopards, tigers, zebras. Cobras came.
He found me brooks and hidden springs.
He taught me lotus and the fringe
Of shadow that will shelter things.
He brought to me what darkness brings.
He gave me bows, and arrow barbs,
My ride, his rein, my name.

Retirement

A Rhyme of the Sad Personal Pronouns

Gathered the rushes
from spring-welled meadows
Gathered the twigs
from a flowering tree
Who was to blame
when the cradles turned brown?

Gathered the bricks
from lands about Sumer
Gathered the timbers
from Lebanon
Who was to blame
when the house fell down?

Gathered the money
from Rome and Lydia
Harappa and Ugarit
Gerza and Thebes
Who was to blame
it cannot buy?

Gathered the tables
from Athens and Golgotha
Gathered the loaves
and the honeyed wine
Who was to blame
if the urns go dry?

Gathered the copper
the tin for casting
Gathered the clay
to build the moulds
Who was to blame
for time and snow?

Gathered the flints
to kindle fire
Gathered the breath
for steady burning
Who was to blame
the way winds blow?

ARTHUR HENRY KING

Death Is the Frame of Love

Death is the frame of love,
our skeletons the groundwork of our play;
and however we move,
the bones move in us that outlast the clay.

Yet bone is a firm ground
to build the highest act of love upon:
if love by death is bound,
it is by limbs in virtue of their bone.

In skull, blade, groin, hip, knee,
we grasp the form that will outlast the eye:
without these dead things we
should not be we to know each other by.

Bone as the frame of love
outlasts the picture. What joy can be there?
Dust the loved self must prove;
but bone framed joy from love's mere flesh and air.

Latter Days

The trees are still in mist this August morning:
chestnut and beech first scorched by sense of Autumn,
and the rest just dull vert between vague seasons.
The swirl of Ceres disciplined to stubble
reduces the whole seasonal cycle's plumed
harvest heads to the rank of interim
waiting empty for the next fulfillment—
presumably the firing of the stubble.

The guns in Hyde Park sound a little distant:
for the Queen-Mother's birthday, not the Queen's;
she came in April, quite a time ago,
an interim.

And fifty-five — since Monday
August the fourth, nineteen-fourteen — brief years
an interim. That was Elizabeth
Bowes-Lyon's fourteenth birthday; a day for call-up
and mobs, not parties; far too large for sickles,
the scale demanded combination harvesters
to reap unseasoned stands in muddy fields.
And yet meanwhile the dragon's teeth sprang wider,
till now the moon can host a bloody harvest.

Back to the trees again! Yes, backs to them,
muffle your eyes in mist! The guns have stopped.
For an interim? Guns, too, are out of season
for execution searing out the scene
from Sandringham to Clarence House or Windsor
and the familiar back-drop
of the once "Great Wen" burst, charred
(unlike Persepolis, past recognition —
granted Macaulay's Antipodean were
conceivable, he drifted Thamesward, and
some local ghost, if even a ghost remained,
could note his pitiless ignorance) — burst, charred,
and year by year barren (of couch, dock, nettle,
or fireweed favoured by a milder Blitz
than this last) — burst, charred, bare, the once Great Wen
that "laughing" corn must wait to "reassume"
                    till the Millennium.

Trees will be lost to site one August morning.

I Will Make Thee a Terror to Thyself (Jer. XX:4)

I have made endeavour to serve thee, Lord,
and yet thy servant—this thy child—
is apprehensive at thy majesty.
Under the blue of day I bow to glory,
acknowledging in gratitude here goodness,
there beauty,
and sometimes the two glancing together;
but, as I drive at night between high mountains
(their summits lost in looming cloud)
or along the edge of some black-aviced lake
(whose unknown depth I hope not accidentally to plumb);
or watch an improbable sea smash up at an impossible cliff;
or even round the zoo (observing
the tiger yawn, the elephant put his foot down,
the octopus tentative, the spider leap,
the fifteen-foot hamadryad
—caught on the Singapore golf-course by coolies who thought him a python—
lunge at the reinforced glass);
or as I await at the clinic, on someone close to me,
a specialist's careful conclusion—
I feel the general terror.

Love beyond, above, and beneath us may
appall us because it exceeds our measure.
Love that creates and includes the predator should
startle us into reconsideration.
Permit us to allow thee
to love and make what thou wilt,
to exercise thine own free agency!

Help me to sense
neither sheer terror nor mere beauty
but both one grace and strength winging the bird of awe
to soar in the courts of thy sublimity.

Aid me to relegate ignoble fear
to the land of that so-called prince of darkness
(for thou art the king of thy deep night
as of thy light, O Christ) —
that pseudo-Lucifer,
who aspired above the aristocracy
and fell to acting the gentleman.

    In the last analysis,
fright turns out to be a kind of
giddiness at the precipices of our own inadequacy,
appears to stalk through
and spring from
our own inner landscape.

It is not what thou has made,
but what we make of ourselves as an interim measure
(for terror can fill any interval
before the apparent ultimate;
and yet that medial "time"
can be "redeemed" from acrophobia):
an interim measure,
a ring of faltering steps
to widen horizons,
reveal peaks further and higher,
open gulfs deeper for thy love to fill:

briefly, to free us from that cozy world
where, each Saturday night,
Father winds the grandfather clock,
then switches off the light,
to release the reign of terror,
the rule of uncomprehended love.

Enable us, therefore, to realize
that we shall continue to render Pan some
breath of involuntary worship,
until we come nearer to understanding

and, yes, matching
thy love.

Hebrews 11: Strangers and Pilgrims

Had we a home elsewhere and chose one here?
From home the stranger makes his crying start:
a touch, a taste, a scent, a voice of dear
concern, a look from eyes to beating heart,
a window on the world. The pilgrim sees
a tree beside a gate; then, many trees.

We take an avenue to find our own;
look for a city — Is our town the place?
We love our country, seek another one;
we gain a wife or husband by thy grace,
a home and children, ours. Away — they've gone
to find their own. Still seeking, we press on.

The valley of the shadow: Lord, thy hand!
We spirit-pilgrims long — in paradise,
yet still on loving earth — for home, a land
of promise and fulfillment. May we rise,
our flesh and bone exalted from the dust,
in that first resurrection of the just!

No longer strange, but pilgrims of that age,
our reunited families can sing,
not solitary on our pilgrimage,
but companied at work for thee our King
a thousand years; till, through refining flame,
one home, all crystal, radiates thy name.

Timpanogos

across the silver
network of birch and poplar
a shiver of gold

MARDEN J. CLARK

To Kevin: Newly a Missionary

You stand before the gates of paradox
In quest for life. You dream deep autumn dreams
Of white: Behold the field. If tares or rocks
Await the sharp-tongued scythe beneath the gleams

Of lives you seek, you'll cut to save your life
But cannot know the life you seek — or yield —
Can only know it lies beyond belief,
Beyond yourself, but somewhere in the field.

I stand behind your dreams and know the tares
And dulling rocks but know the Rock. And know
How flaming tongues will help in finding yours,
How much of you must edge into the flow

Of self that harvests precious heads of grain
Including yours: A tongue rock-blunt and plain.

August 6

"Go get dressed. You're no man for this army!"
I went, thanking for the first time that crook
In my spine that had stopped me buck naked
From buck privacy, had taken me back to you
After a three-hour, not a three-year, separation.

Together we heard the celebration:
Hiroshima Wiped Out! With one bomb!
With one bomb! Now the war will have to end!
We celebrated with the rest. Celebrated the bomb,
Celebrated rejection, celebrated your birthday, my love.

For forty years now, to celebrate your birthday
We've had to celebrate the bomb, but on
A sliding scale: from first exuberance
To slow knowing to terror now. Your poor birthday,
Growing on an opposing scale, tonight
Gets only a bad movie as celebration.

The spine that bought my rejection
Has cost me plenty since in pain, but none
Like that of the bomb I failed to feel as pain.

"The crowning savagery of war!" J. Reuben Clark
Called those bombs. But we dismissed him:
Old and embittered. I'm old and bitter now.
I call him back to witness — against me,
Against all who would not hear, who do not hear.

The speed of light squared! That bomb still lives,
Mushrooming in our memories, a ghost in the galaxy
A thousand times alive in its sleek rude brood
Begotten of that equation
On technology, the mushroom prefiguring
And portending, Cassandra-like, the progeny
Expanding at the square of the speed of light.

Ah, love, let us be true . . . The ebb and flow
Are sucking and swelling to a tidal wave!
Our leaders run like children
Down the sand in the deep ebb sucked out
By the coming wave, like children down the sand
To pluck for their crowns the shining baubles
Bared before the wave.

We love. That may be all we do or have
When the wave bursts over us.
And if the voice of apocalypse be not heard
We must at least let the silent waves of our love
Be known: We love.

Joseph's Christmas Eve

Seems almost Jahveh didn't want us here.
    Feet sore enough to make me etch
In slow relief each rock and tree. Even now
    Could I have doubts so great they'd stretch

The road like that? or drag us finally here
    To where no door will close against
The cold, where (father, no father) I've straw for ease
    Of pangs — they seize her now! — where scents

Are stench of barn and stall? The simple ass
    That carried her deserves as much.
What word was that? Only a cry newborn.
    And what a cry! So soon. The touch

Of Mary's breath tonight meant heaven's close.
    And now that light above the ridge,
That choir, both softly swelling softly filling
    As if with light and sound to bridge

The earth and sky. Look! They come to rest
    On Mary's berth, reflecting clear
As though that manger were their source. It is:
    The Word himself, Jahveh, lies here.

Wasatch

Whose fault lies here and subtly traces
Limits of an ancient sea whose waves
Lapped softly over desert sands
To front abruptly mountain faces

We still see and climb? What hands
Thrust plate against then under plate
To slowly toss, to lightly toss
Such mountains up? Who understands

Tectonic forces that could freight
America five thousand miles
And gently spread Atlantic where
No waters were? What sun of late

Could swiftly shrink that sea to glare
Salt flat white or shimmer-sheen
Salt-water blue and leave behind
These loam-spread fields? What people here

With ox or hand or power unseen
Crossed wilderness then crossed these heights
Built cities here to front this fault
And find in valleyed walls their dream

Of refuge fully filled? What refuge here
For us as we look up in awe
And love to these high peaks? Whose fault
If now these plates again should stir?

EDWARD L. HART

To Utah

I. Arrival

Nobody wanted this place:
Spaniards saw it and turned back;
Trappers endured the taste
Of salt in the wind for the fur pack
Or love of space.

When settlers planned
Westward treks it was California
They chose, and cursed this land
For standing in the way with its thorns and
Hot sand.

The sun of a late July
Burns varnish onto summit rock.
Wagons and teams go by.
Escarpments for a moment block
The scalding sky.

Teams trail in a line now,
Over the downward roll of the hill,
Brushed by cedar bough;
Then ages of Indian stone worlds spill
From an iron plow.

II. Laying out the City

A sextant captures a light train
Bounced from the moon to a Great Basin
Point where Brigham Young's cane
Marks the site for the temple mason.

Rays of base lines running through
South Temple and Main embrace
The cosmos in a grid beginning at a new
Meridian of time and space.

III. The Gathering

They came by thousands at a slow clip,
All but those buried at Haun's Mill
Or Florence or some place that the lip
Of man had no name for yet to trip
The tongue of the young, who wanted still
To find home over the next hill
Or lush pastures past each desert strip.

They came over the mountains and around
The Horn in ships and wagons, or dragged
Handcarts over stony and frozen ground,
Often opened and shovelled in a mound
Upon women and children or the man who lagged
In his shafts only on the day he sagged
In death on the crosspiece: Zion bound.

IV. Preparing for Fire

Leaving the City

You build a city and leave it, maybe
To burn. All morning wagons piled
Full have gone by to the south,
And now we leave our house with straw
Stacked in the doorway, ready for fire.
Where we go next, who knows?
Sonora, maybe: it's a long way.

Instructing the Torchbearers

Then it's settled; you know the signal.
The city burns if only one soldier
Steps out of line or raises his hand
As a vandal or takes for his own use
One spoon or disturbs a stick of kindling.
Soldiers will not tie our hands
Here and hold us tamely for mobs
To rub in the dust again: never.
Joseph's body was propped by a pump
As a target for soldiers sent to protect him
From themselves. Before that happens
Here we'll level the city with fire
And leave them the ashes of our past.

General Albert Sidney Johnston Marches through Salt Lake City

The naked bayonets of the Fifth
Infantry flash in the van of the Union
Army in morning sunshine. Baggage
Wagons and caissons still rumbling
At dusk through deserted streets send
Echoes rattling from locked and hollow
Houses to the valley walls while
Crickets shrill in cadence from the hills.

V. Expansion

Any of a hundred places: name it
And go there and try to claim it
From Indians and insects, rodents and drouth.
Try, for instance, going south
To Pipe Spring, in the northern strip
Of Arizona above the ripped
Rock at Grand Canyon and stay
For years, two hundred miles away
From a boy who'd ask your boy to play.

VI. Temple

Cradled in world-weighted darkness
The core cooled slowly and granite grew
Into flecks of mica and pods of quartz
Around flowering feldspar and hornblende.
Weathering winds and rains cut off
Soft cover; light glinted
From orthoclastic patterns as quarrying
Frost pried free a block at last
To stand capstone at the temple crest.

Winter

As usual: six, and we dressed,
But the sky was still dark until seven.
Morning was grim in the west;
Summer was gone by eleven.

Nobody spoke at chores.
When we finished, we bedded the stables,
Chinked the cracks in the gables,
And bolted the granary doors.

The lawn was the first spot white.
Stubble was covered by noon.
In evening's feeble light
Earth lay in a marble swoon.

And then the wind woke with a roar
That hollowed our house like a cave.
Night rolled from the hills in a wave
And swallowed the world to our door.

Spring

Spring came slowly to the valley lands,
Slower to the hills
Where pines unmortised from their melting molds
Slipped dripping loads,
And their glistening needles, wetwaxed, glared.
Ice on the creek
Quit cracking, crashing caves of crystals,
Soon resumed
The rumble and the rush of far-off feud.
A dark town
Cowered in the canyon mouth between
The hills' knees,
Its bare trees bristling like a ruffled bird's
Plumes. The all
But inaudible sound of the sinking snow
Stirred wonder without words
In us. We forsook the long wan winter's
Bound encumbrance
And felt the unfettered freedom of the live
Loadlifted limbs.

The Launching

The gyroscope in the skull wobbles eccentric
To a tilt, skidding satellite eyes off orbit
And smashing aspic ears into ions of time
As massed critical speed in the wake of a shrill
Screaming pulse careens the head to wreck,
Leaving the apple rotting in the neck.

Depletion

The city darkens with the natural night
Like country houses when the twilight ends
On summer evenings and no form unbends
From strain of too much day to make more light.

New York Provincial

"Now this poem is about seagulls," she said;
"No one in Utah would understand, of course"
(So condescending, Charlotte said of Darcy's aunt);
"Seagulls belong in Brooklyn or Staten Island."
I've seen her with a dozen faces:
Once she was the little man from Harvard
At the navy language school in Colorado.
He was lost anywhere except Boston—but Boulder!
The desolation of the Great Plains and the chaos
Of the Rocky Mountains confounded him. He was the one
That got drunk, vomited in the hall and slept
While the rest of us cleaned up because no one
Would tell on him. Later, in Honolulu, he did
The honorable thing, a harakiri job on himself,
And went to a Boston heaven.
She was in England too once—a female impersonator
This time. She asked my wife on a big red London
Bus if in Utah we got married in the nude.
I was even her once myself, when invited
By a Muslim friend to hunt wild pigs in Pakistan.
What do you do with them after, I asked. Eat them?
"Imagine," she is saying of her poem—the one
We won't understand—"a seagull." Our state bird,
I tell her. "You mean eagle," she assured me.

IRIS PARKER CORRY

The Year of the Famine

When the iron works was shutting down
and you couldn't buy a sack of flour
in Cedar Valley at any price
(grasshoppers we had—but no gulls),
the Lord sent mushrooms.

Outside the town they umbrellaed
on the black creek bank
and in scant shade—
everywhere the benign toadstools.
Mornings we gathered them—always enough.
For Sunday dinner a little flour
to thicken the juice, and pigweed greens.

In the fall an abundance of
honeydew fell on the willows.
We fetched washtubs and other vessels
and rinsed the branches in water
and it boiled down
to the beautifullest syrup I ever tasted.

In the year of the famine, 1856.

Nellie Unthank

aged ten,
walked, starved, froze
with the Martin Company
and left her parents in shallow graves
near the Sweetwater.

The Richards on First South
hugged their children's heads to muffle
Nellie, strapped to a board, without anesthetic,
screaming, her frost-black feet
removed with a butcher knife
and a carpenter's saw.

After that she walked on her knees,

married in polygamy to
William Unthank (of Cedar City)
who took her home to one room with a dirt floor.
She damped and scraped that floor
hard and smooth as sandstone,
washed it every day;
clean muslin curtains at the window,
on goods box cupboards.

Saturday nights the hearth whitened
and Nellie made her way
knitting, crocheting, carding wool,
kneeling by the washtub set on blocks
scrubbing townspeople's clothes on the board
and trading a yeast start for
a handful of sugar sent in the jar.

Said *never* to another operation —
waddled on leather kneepads in her little skirt
dragging her unhealed stumps
or pushed herself on a board on wheels.

Once a year Nellie and her six children cleaned
the meeting house.
The boys fetched water;
Annie, Martha, Polly washed the windows.
Nellie scrubbed the floor.

Lovers at Twilight

A distinction may be made between the two.
She rests her head on his shoulder, shifting
Her lightness nearer to him, and he, lifting
Her hand from the bench, and wondering who
He might be to deserve her, considers anew
Her languor of ease, her comfort close by,
Almost nodding, nearly asleep, knowing why
She is so, that he has found her in lieu
Of anyone else, and she of course him, forever.
And such involvement, like orbiting suns
Of space gleaming or winking, in their shire
Of silences, strands of light no one can sever,
Extending forever! What is it in them that stuns
The will awake to attend what never will tire
In the chasm of night?

Advent

The gentle God is our guest;
His staff will prompt us to the door.

The table is set in the oak-paneled room:
Goblets are rinsed and set out,
The warm vapor vanishing around them;
The silver, withdrawn from felt-lined red mahogany,
Is counted and burnished to mercurial white
And set on immaculate linen,
Sleek with crystal and rococo ware.

The table is set for the Guest
Near the imminent door.
The servants stalk
Each gray indiscretion to be rent
On the merciless rack of their decor.

The table is set for the gentle God:
The roasted fowl entice the savoring tongue;
The marmalade and sweetmeats brim
The centerpiece, a horn;
The fruit is full, plucked in prime,
Oranges, apples, pears
Like noon-shade autumn leaves.
The supper will please the gentle God
Who surely comes,
Who comes like the breath on a veil.

But out of the East the breath is fire!
Who comes with temblor, sound of hurricane?
Who rages on the portico?
Who claps his vengeful steel on stone?
Who comes to dine?

The servants cower like quail in the anterooms.
Who blasphemes in the shuddering halls?
Who rends the imminent door?
Our guest is a gentle God, a Lamb.

To a Dying Girl

How quickly must she go?
She calls dark swans from mirrors everywhere:
From halls and porticos, from pools of air.
How quickly must she know?
They wander through the fathoms of her eye,
Waning southerly until their cry
Is gone where she must go.
How quickly does the cloudfire streak the sky,
Tremble on the peaks, then cool and die?
She moves like evening into night,
Forgetful as the swans forget their flight
Or spring the fragile snow,
So quickly she must go.

Jesse

We stumbled up the stairs, onto the back porch,
Where Jesse's father kept his hunting gear,
His shotgun leaning against a porch screen
That puffed a mist of dust when touched or rubbed.
So Jesse said, "Look out. The step is loose."
We went in, asking his mother, Leah, for time
To ride out to the lake. With her assent,
We left, grazing the evening with whispering,
And threw blankets over the horses whose reins
We left slack to the ground. We steadied them
And jumped up easily, jostling and settling
Where best to ride. Then off into the evening,
Wresting from the near air intimacy and warmth
Of summer. And we rode down the even lane,
Grass and darkness to either side, the katydids

Sounding over the rhythm of the horses we kept
In the surer way, peering somberly as we went.
Jesse felt the defection from day and the tug
Of seeming to have lost it so early, after play.
He said: "The day was short enough; evening
Brings the sound of water up the shining sand.
Let's see, tonight, how high the dark lakewater
Must rise to touch the willows on the shore
Where the inlet keeps its secrecy." I nodded,
Softly yielding to the restraint of solemnity,
Reaching forward to the mane for firm balance.
I said, "A rift of light rests forward here.
Let's follow it." And he replied, "I find
The sallow world at the far edge of my hand,
And the restless rainwind veers across the lake.
I left my father and mother in the livingroom
Wondering why I leave them, even with you.
Questions glanced across their faces like shadows
Of boughs lifting in the breeze of evening.
I should return. But the leafing air grazes
My loneliness. Out there, where the evening
Fails, stars appear in the dark paling sky
Like memory returning." And we rode silently
As I heard the grasses against the hooves,
Near the lake. And I saw the lancet dark
Invade the gloss of water and the rippling light.
I looked at him askance and saw his eyes
And the gild of water draw a shining sleep
Into them. And as we returned, he softly rehearsed
The gentle inflections of light he knew. He said,
"I know the prince that stands beyond the air."

And afterwards, when in England I caught news
Of him in the random vision of words in print,
Newsprint fragile and yellowing as it seemed
To slip and fall from an envelope, I knew
He stumbled from step to porch, near the screen,
And jarred the bluesteel set of hammer and shank
That his father had left for his quick return.
And at once I felt the slow gait of the horses
Near the lake, where the lights of evening ease
And whisper into being beyond the gloss of day.

Arab Insurrection: A Memoir

White as stone, he sits agape in a chair,
Tassels of willows beyond, sweeping the air.
Daylight, a bright thinness fair

As gauze, intervenes. He sits, tipping
Into it, to see: Algiers — the sipping
Of wine in a portico, swallows nipping

At cherries in the dry wind, the aeration
Of sight, straws and shadows in an adumbration
Of belief, his wife at the gate to hear elation

In the streets. Allah, in shadows, comes
Turbaned and flowing in robes, his thumbs
Dismaying her. Great with child, she drums

The light with horror as a scimitar, against the gate,
Cleaves its grain. The latch falls charily, late
As a golden minaret to seize the sun. I wait

To see him see, white of stone, remembering:
Like a brown wind, they sweep against her, dismembering
Her fingers before him, the spurt of blood tempering

Their steel. In a flourish of will, they stare
At him, but turn to her to split and pare
Her like a gourd, the foetus bloody and fair

In their hands, slowly appearing. In the bright essence
Of day, he rocks stonily, seeing, his sense
Failing, gathering and picking, in a prescience

Of death, pictures in the air. They fill
Her with the stones they threw and kneel to kill
Her veins that pulse in dust as they will

Him as he is, rocking in a chair, their whim
Always before him, endlessly wavering and dim.

Homestead in Idaho

I

"Solomon? Since I talked with him I've thought
Again about trying to make a go of it
In Idaho. As I say, this rainy weather
In Oregon is looking better and better to me.
The first time I met him, it was in Al's Bar,
Down the street. Five years ago, I think.
Well, you know, Al keeps a friendly place,
One where you don't mind stepping in
And acting neighborly. Well, there he was,
Down at the end of the bar. I noticed him
Because he was shaking, folding and unfolding a clipping.
'You from these parts?' I said. With all this space
In the West, it doesn't hurt to close it up
Whenever you can. He said, 'Well, no, not really,'
And kept folding and unfolding the clipping and looking
Down at his hands. When he stopped, I could hardly
See it, his hands were so square and big,
Like the farm work of his time. Besides, he took
His hat off, and you could see the white skin
Of his head, particularly near the part,
Where his hat took a settled, permanent place.
But his face had lightened to a buckskin color.
He had the look of a farmer who had seen a lot
Of land that needed working. Then it rose
From him. 'I suppose you would say from Idaho.
I wanted to homestead there,' he said. 'I tried it
Last year, or was it then? Not much money
To start with, but my wife Geneva and I and our children
Found a place. But it seemed a thousand miles
Fom nowhere, at least two weeks east from here.
I built a cabin from the boards I had brought
Along. Geneva said, 'Solomon, we can make it,
But we need money for spring. Go back to Tamarack
And leave us here.' Then I told her how I felt.
But she said, 'We can make it with the provisions we brought.
Go back, Solomon. By spring, we'll have a start,
Then a barn by those trees, cows grazing there,

And a house like we've wanted, beside a stream.'
Well, the way she looked, her eyes imploring,
And her soft brown hair, and her hope, how could I
Say no? So off I went, Geneva waving to me
Until I was out of sight. It was the hardest thing
I have ever done to look around and see
Where I was going. I worked at Tamarack
Autumn and winter, numb from wondering
How they were, all alone out there, and wanting
To get back to them. April finally came,
And I loaded the wagon with everything we needed,
Dresses and dry goods, shoes and ribbons besides.
I travelled as hard as I could, considering the horses,
And kept looking and looking for the smoke far off
In front of me, coming from the chimney,
To tell me I was near. But I never saw it.'
He looked again at the clipping in his hands,
Smudged and yellow, and said, 'When I got there,
It looked like autumn and winter had never left,
The snow still hanging on the roof, the door
Open, nothing planted, nothing done,
And then I went inside, to see the dusty cribs
And Geneva, still against them . . . and the floor
Red and dusted with shadows. And I was here,
Trying for money so we could get started. . . .
I couldn't stay out there.' And he looked at me
As if pleading for help, then down into his hands,
Unfolding and folding the clipping as if by doing it
He could wear out his sorrow."

II

The colors of the sun against the hills
In the evensong of life, and yet another
Year had gone. The colors crept down
Like frost and the glory of God, intermingling
In them night and day. All was over
When the family saw them, over like the evening
Wind. In the meadows and clusters of pines
It whispered to the edge of the sullen earth,
In the seethe of knowing, under the shaken plume

Of knowledge. Solomon and Geneva saw
The land cut, as it were, for them, a place
For them between the great divide and the sea.
There, he said in the voice of conscience, there
Is our home, or the hope of it. Geneva,
Can it be that home if we settle here?
A half of a year will make it ours if we stay,
She replied in the moment of seeing him
As she wished him to be. And then in resolve,
Let me stay the winter with the children
While you work in Tamarack, and so
It was out, the only way of keeping
The land. Where in the flicker of grey is death,
The wandering light, release? I want this home,
She said, in the tolerance of a breath, and I
Shall stay. Where is the imperious will but fast
Against the land that holds them? To Tamarack,
He said, bright as possession, like the coin of having
Mastery. There is my knoll where home
Shall be, not this cabin of our duration
As we should not be, itinerants in hope of more.
A winter more, she said, and it is ours,
The gaze of meadows, the water and soil
Urgent for grain, the quiet sky, and the light
Lazy as spring. Our home! And I shall keep it,
Winter through, she said, as if it were no winter,
But a day of rest. And then beside him, their children,
Or in his arms, awake to happiness. The future
Declined from that day and would not rest,
But as a bole of pain grew into that tower
Of resolve and broke it easily, sacred
As a sacrifice. He said, then think of me
In Tamarack, and turned to what he needed
Away from home. Geneva? The subtle portrait
On a stand beside a bed. The wisps
Of hair she flicked to clear her face, brown
As the veil of earth, eyes quizzical as worry,
But light as a soft morning, her body lithe
And restless, supple to the rule of God.
And Solomon? A name like a fetish he tried
To honor, but not as a patriarch, more
Like a seer: angular as a fence or cross,

Bending as he seemed to fit, concern
Like an agony to please, a burden
To his clothes that could not shape themselves,
And altogether like the square largeness
Of his hands. Together, they kept the cabin
Like a tidy loom where they would weave
The colors through their bright fidelity.
Their children? Hard to presuppose or know,
But theirs. Such small alliances, wont
To shimmer with translucent light, a guess
Of women that might have been, of course like her,
Or him, as others might suppose, not they.
She whispered what he might take, advice.
Hanging from her words like surety.
And he, the slight concerns of food and health
Like the hundreds of miles that would intervene,
And for safety the gun and knife in a drawer,
Nearby. Then the wood for winter near the door,
Neatly stacked, and provisions in the loft
And ready. What else? What else but land
Beyond their vision, the canyons, and peaks like clouds
In the thin blue haze, and time. He turned, ready,
Holding her with one arm, as he pulled
His horse from grazing to the suggestion of the miles
Ahead, and leaned to kiss his children, and then
Away, easily in the saddle, gazing back at her,
The children, cabin, everything diminishing
As he moved, and he waved, and they, in the slow
Desperation of goodbye. He could not turn forward
For seeing them there, until they were taken from view
By a vale beyond their meadow sinking into darkness,
And they were gone. From that time on he pieced
The events of time together like fragments he could not
Understand, though the evidence impaled the past
Like needles dropping suddenly through his inquiry.
There must have been a disturbance beyond the door,
And she left the cabin with the gun on her arm.
The sharp wind of October against her frailty
Where she shivered in the grey dusk. The rising
Wind, then the thunder over the plain that shook her.
She went into the darkness of a shed, wildly
Gazing. Then the severe and immediate rattle
Behind her, and the strike behind her knee, the prongs

Of venom there that made her scream. Now
The whirling thoughts for Solomon or help
From anywhere. Bleed the poison out.
Go slowly, she told herself, and bleed the poison
Out. Stumbling to the cabin, she opened the door
In the glaze of fright and found the drawer that held
The knife. She sat, livid against the lightning,
To find the place to cut. Nowhere to see,
Behind and under, but she felt the red periods there.
A piece of kindling for a brace, a cloth
For tourniquet. She took the knife and swept it
With her hand. But the chickens in the shed.
They must not starve. A few steps back
To the shed, and she emptied a pail of grain
And opened the door. As she moved, she held
The stick of the tourniquet numbly against her leg.
Slowly, slowly to the cabin, then wildly in
To seize the knife. She held it against her leg
And with a gasp twisted it in. But too deep!
The blood pulsed against her hand, again,
Again, no matter how tightly she twisted the stick
To keep it in. It spread on the rough floor
As she felt herself weaken, the waves of blackness
Before her eyes. The children! What will happen
To them? she cried to herself. The lamp flickered
At the sill. What good is the need and planning now?
Tears for dust. The girls will starve to death
In the clatter of the wind, and the light of afternoon
Will carve through their sallow loneliness.
They will lie here and cry for food, and no one will hear.
The waning fire, the gusts at the filming window.
Solomon! Forgive me! What can I do?
What else can I do? She took the gun again
And turned it to the crib, propping its weight.
She looked at them as they slept, arms lightly
Across each other. You will be with me,
She whispered to them. The trigger once, then again,
The flat sounds walling her against the error
That they would live beyond her careful dying.
The gun fell from her. She crawled to the bed
In the corner and, taking her finger, traced
In blood on the white sheet, "Rattlesnake bit,

Babies would star—" and the land fell away
Beyond her sight, and all that she was collapsed
In an artifice of death that he afterwards saw.
Solomon!

The Death of Ramses II

Like droplets from a clock, or rain,
    Time comes, descending over me.
    Drafts of light pass over the sea
To reside in a tomb and in the pain

Of memory. They pass and are gone,
    But shelter still another day. O sun,
    Your rays enfold and fade in dun
Sand, but make it gold. Upon

My sepulchre so shine to be
    Remembered so in me. Circle
    My life with gold, before death's sickle,
As if with wheat, and over the sea

Of sky where then I may embark
    With remembrances in the hush of time.
    I keep these artifacts like thyme
In my devotion. Not on the stark

Night river may I pass, but on the golden
    Shimmer I see like the molten
    Sun that blesses me. Distant, unspoken,
And unspeaking Thou in the fold

Of your eternal day. I keep
    My cartouche near unto the height
    Of heaven in the haven of your might.
Transform my Egypt, and me, before I weep

To feel my passing into the silent tomb.

EMMA LOU THAYNE

Love Song to the End of Summer

It is clear now, body. Every day can be late August,
after the birth of babies, never quite cold.

But one must learn early what you are for forever.

Good old leather tiger, half domesticated
by paws in pans and shoulders hung too often with beaded fur,
you may think I forget. But you do not let me.
By now I know better. I come back.

Still, you never take me not surprised, faithful one,
by how to arrive, and the pleasure of sweat,
and how to shiver away the bee.
You move to the song behind the dance,
Even after a standard, plain white, unstriped day,
you ripple in our sleep and wait, mostly unperplexed.

And when no matter how faint, the music breathes
behind the catcalls of too much to do, you muster
almost without my inclining, potent as needing to dance,
to pace off the house, the garden of weeds, the clogged creek,
and the midnight clutch of vagrancies. You pad from
some spring and, wild, except for my importuning,
go. To do it all.

When we lie down, it will be like the squirrel there,
unflagging in the last swift moving in the leaves,
August stashed in crisp piles above the dust.

I may find no way at all without your sleek taking.

Under the wrinkles that tell you no, I can hear you now
saying, "I still love you," and to time, "Leave her alone."

Considering — the End

So finally I consider only life: The holocaust ahead
would leave no one behind
to question how we happened not to happen
in any moment but our tragic own.

I have only one voice, one language,
one set of memories to look back on,
a thousand impulses to look ahead
if I will
if there is time
to consider:
How much for the earth?
what would I keep?

Blue mountains against a black sky,
Smiles exchanged so well we do not know our ages or conditions.

Snow melted, leaves moving again,
In a voice, rain finding its way to the stream.

Heat rising like wands from the desert,
A cold drink, the touch of hair enough all by itself.

First apricot pickle sharp, a phone ringing on time,
Lights going on, wanting them off for the dark.

A song flooded with memory, smell of piñon in fire, onion in stew,
A dancer watched like a child, a child in flight like a dancer.

Hot soup, hot bath, hot air to take to the canyon,
Aging slowly from the bones outward, time to pick and choose.

A wooden spoon, the white whisper of a needle in cloth,
Laughing like tossed water, like skis on snow.

Smell of soap, hot animal. An apple, crisp. A ball hit,
Tongue of a lover, dream of a dead mother stroking our cheek.

An idea, the Pietà, the Hand of God, a word, a prayer,
The word, the earth far from without form and void.

The earth created and not destroyed. If altered,
Not back to darkness upon the face of the deep.

You, me, combinations of color and sound,
The spirit of God moving upon the waters.

A child born, an aunt with reason to blow draw blow,
A celebration for the end of war. A new generation inevitable.

The coming of sun because it is good.
A world alive for a blue door to open onto.

A candle, a kiss, eyes meeting. Holding.
Life — to consider.

Then no more considering, hypothesizing, tolerating.

No litmus-paper ending in a cosmic Petri dish.

No more silence.

For the earth?

For the life in me, in you,
I say Yes. Yes thank you. Yes.

In your breath fused with mine
Even ashes stir and glow.

It's time. It's time we said together
Yes to life. To ashes, simply No.

Woman of Another World, I Am with You

You, woman of different tongue,
awaken me.

Speak in the language of light
that flutters between us.
Open my heart to your dailiness;
give voice to your fears and celebrations
as you wonder at mine.

Your family becomes me,
the substance of what you believe
colors my view.
You take me on.

Here, here is my hand.
Filled with yours
it pulses with new hope
and a fierce longing
to let the light that guides us both
tell me where to be.

Massada

The remaindering of zeal is more than irresistible.
Those Jews still occupy the fragments
of Herod's ample auspices.

On this place of daggers and stallions
they cry out for stabbings
on the blind stairways. Their deft watches
startle the split storehouses. A galloping
stuns the marble overlooking the sheer drop
that if kept an altar, left them
isolate and ready as a thundercloud.

The air is still pungent with raw
suggestion and heady with Eleazar striding
across conscience, collecting pulses,
denying by some intimate fuse the pillage —
and the promise? There is a shuffling
of systems, the drawing of means.
Rape and reduction are staved off as
they are accomplished.

Charged with triumphant carnage,
perverse, the particles of a private
holocaust wound the stones to keep
the gusts of life unsullied over
the Dead Sea.

As the tram rides its thick wire up for the view.

To a Daughter about to Become a Missionary
For Dinny

Twenty-two, she sleeps upstairs
between the windows of my life,
in the sleigh bed that has housed
the comings of four generations

like exotic potted plants chosen
to color bedrooms with blossoming.
Two high birdseye dressers contain her,
drawers closed on pink turtle-necks

and speedos, walls of rackets and mustachioed
smiles. Mirrors swing her reflection
of medicated soap and squashed rollers
dropping away from night to issue

a daytime Pietà laughing and grieving,
beautifully turned out, surprising as
a crocus in snow. Other rights postponed,
the child that God intended will wear

the sanctity of the blue blazer,
skirted and frocked, innocent in her
expectation. Of course we have known
she would leave, the covers

opened and closed. It is time.
The horizon whitens. Water runs.
This is morning. She will see. France
will tell. She is changing to

the garments of The Word, will take on
the terrors of the verb To Be,
not knowing yet why departure
spells return. Five-hundred forty-seven

and a half days. She will open wide
her arms sweatered for the long cold.
The darkness will lighten and she will become
the waiting room for the willing stranger.

Kisses blow like blizzards through my empty
spaces saying God, please. I go up to sit on
her suitcase that will not close,
press messages into her shoes,

the smell of kitchen under the leather
of her scriptures. Snow has made feathers
of trees. She lifts the sleepy shadow
of her face, steps into the air. She is gone.

I do not dare breathe in the bedroom.
Or move. Only to listen to the runners
of the sleigh bed following her.

And me unable to make it for fear
of blanketing the sweet shiny smell
of Dr. Pepper lip gloss beneath the down,
above the furrows of knees along the floor.

JOHN STERLING HARRIS

Fallow

She eased herself into the bed beside him,
His farmer's heavy sleep
Was lighter now with dawning near.
At the creak of springs
He stirred
And turned to reach her hand, holding it,
Carefully as his calloused fingers would allow.

Have you been up to make the fire, Jennie?
She caught her breath and held her answer,
But in a moment said,
I rose to find the crop you planted failed
Like the others—this field lies fallow still.

He took his turn at delay
And reached to pull her in before reply.
Perhaps I planted too shallow
Or in the wrong time of moon
Or worse, the seed was old and weak—
You haven't yourself to blame for that.
A man can't really know the cause in this.
I've wondered at it though.

If it came from a boyhood fever—
The men at the blacksmith shop
Would call it shooting blanks
Or some such thing,
And laugh and say that
If a man's father had no sons,
It's likely he won't either.
I've never thought it could be you—
Not with your sister's brood,
And your twin brother's wife
Is walking heavy now.

Stop, she said, Can't you see.
A freemartin heifer never calves.
Some places, you know, you could
Send me back like faulty goods,
And well you should.
I've seen you envy other men their sons.
And I know about that shiny
Pony saddle in the barn.
If you had another woman—

A Hagar to dam an heir, he said.
And watch you go to quiltings
So you can tend the children there
And have to listen to
The smug complaints of overbearing wives,
And then return to your
Own quiet house to weep.

No, I'll not have that.
We need not wait for spring,
And if the field does not reject
The plow, we'll plant again.

The field does not reject the plow
Till gulls no longer follow in the furrow,
But with this latest loss
The plowing seems a ritual now
Of some forgotten faith
Or a prayer to a departed god.
But it comforts those that live,
When all the meaning's gone.

E. H. 1817

It looks like any framing square
Twenty-four inches on the stock
Eighteen on the leg
I'm told twice-great grandfather Emer
Forged it from a sword,
And it bears his mark — E.H. 1817.

The numbers and the marks are faint
But readable still
When you slant it to the light
To show the dents of hammer blows.

The graduations are widespread —
No subtleties beyond a quarter inch —
But I cannot fault their accuracy
With the finest modern scale.

They say he used it in the building
Of the temple at Nauvoo —
I wonder where his compass is —
And Brigham had him
Build a ferry too
At the last crossing of the Platte.

With it he built the house
And the Church at Clarkston,
And his son built at Alpine and Monroe
And his at Payson and Colonia Juarez and Cardston
And his at Logan and Richmond and Tooele —
Scattered places on a western map —
New towns with straight streets
And square corners.

It leans by the bookshelf now —
An heirloom, a conversation piece for show.
But its angle is true —
If it were needed
For the building of New Jerusalem.

Hay Derrick

You can see the derrick there
In the lower meadow by the marsh
Where there's a low stack
Of hay against the pale sky.

The father made them unhook the chain
That linked the pole to base
And lowered the end
To rest upon the ground.

But the big pine pole
Used to point toward the sun like a dial
And swing across a summer sky
To raise the loads of meadow hay

That creaking wagons brought to the stack—
The Jackson hanging from the block,
With four curved tines like blades of scythes
Dropping down and sinking in the load,

Then hoisting high with cable taut,
Turning slowly in the air,
And swinging over the stack
With the screek of straining blocks—

Then the shout of *yo* to pull
The trip rope and dump the hay,
Returning then to the wagon—
Eight forkfulls for the load.

So they were that August day,
The father pushing the fork into the load,
His son carefully building the stack,
And a child on the plodding derrick horse

That drew the cable up
Then backed to let it down,
In easy rhythm of lower
And hoist and swing and drop.

Then there came a shift of wind
That made the derrick horse start.
The child tried to pull the reins,
But the horse bolted fast.

The empty fork flew to the block
But stopped and then plunged down
Where one tine pinned the son to the stack
And the broken cable covered him with coils.

They left the stack unfinished
To bleach in the summer sun,
And the autumn winds stirred the hay
Like unkempt hair on the head of a boy.

Tag, I. D.

Bright oval on a light chain,
Last name first,
Then Christian name
And middle initial,
A number assigned by a master,
A letter for his blood,
Another for his god—
Tooth-notched
Stainless steel coin
For the boatman.

Apprentice

While yet a boy he learned his father's trade—
Watching the scribe of the compass arc,
Standing in the sawpit with dust in his eyes,
Swinging the adze to cut to the line,
Holding the chisel tight under mallet blows
Against the crooked grain of olive wood,
Fitting the tenon close and locking it
With hammered pegs in augured holes,
Plumbing the post, leveling the beam and
Setting the latch—he mastered it all.

He left that trade to teach—
To mark the line
And hew men's lives—
Till lifted up on post and beam,
He hung upon the nails
And showed he knew his Father's trade.

DAVID L. WRIGHT

The Conscience of the Village
from River Saints — Introduction to a Mormon Chronicle

His eyes milky, intensely blue,
Fasten totally upon the life that was living
From 1884 to nineteen hundred and twelve;
Not seeing the life that has been his dying since,
Though he has braked the crawl toward surcease
More courageously successful than we (even I, the Valley's Poet)
In our existing.
Now, in the final year of his dying, unfamiliar people,
Like Sadie his long-suffering, gentle wife,
Plunge his hat on his head and speak of things
(Eat your bread, Father, then we'll help you to the bathroom)
Having nothing to do with the untranslatable essence
Of those Maori days worshipping with savages who loved him,
And the boyhood before it, fishing the river,
Talking with God,
They — Sadie, his son Nathan, his granddaughters (two) —
Occupants and masters of his home now,
Caution him, watch your step, Father,
Sit down, shut up the girls are studying,
Try not to cry, Father, sleep well, Father,
We know what's best for you,
Hushing his twanging outbreaks of Maori war and wedding chants,
The sharp-syllabled cries likely to disturb or frighten
The granddaughters, who must study and listen to
The Beatles.
(:Well, what are they doing here anyhow? This is my house)
(:Shhhh, Father, you're not well . . . behave yourself . . .
You wouldn't want us to take you to Blackfoot would you?)
At which mention of Idaho's mental institution
He cries,
Crumbling the bread on the oilcloth,
Sipping water (perhaps in remembrance of his blood?)
And wipes his nose with a middle finger large
With arthritis, its joint broken by a kicking hog,
Thirty years ago, in the middle of the dying time;
Now guiding that finger to grasp at crumbs,

(*Surely*, the Poet thinks, in remembrance of the Lord).

Sadie saying: now Father . . .
Gently washes his hands with a washrag
:Your friend is here, you haven't
Seen him since he went away.
But he cries still, his head bobbing to table's edge,
His hand uncaring loose
In the kindly grasp of his long-suffering
Who endured and never blamed him for their children's rags
Throughout the carefree, dying years.
:Father! Don't you remember?
Carl's son . . . he's coming to see you.
He turns his milky eyes up, his lips form, break,
And re-form angles over the cavern of mouth
:Carl's Boy?
? . . . ?
Yes, yes . . .
For the Poet heard and saw the Maori world,
As a village boy listened and seemed
To understand
The war and wedding chants:
Saw empathetically, visions and remembrances,
As they were—
Of young Mormon missionary, Matthew Daniels,
Baptizing natives in fish-filled streams,
Eating ceremonial trout,
Tempted by but not submitting to barebreasted daughters
Of the chief
Because of Judith, his village sweetheart,
In the days of living when vows were not mired
In the moss of lust.
Saw too, himself pleading for more tales,
More songs, more images of rivers and oceans
Aborigines paint-smeared and loin-cloth
Naked—
Saw too the young Matthew equally vermillion and naked,
Dancing chanting with them,
Like one of them—
Saw too his leading the chief
Into the river,
Baptizing him in the name of God, Son, and Holy Ghost,

Not insisting as all missionaries were ordered
That the otherwise pure in heart
Must discontinue smoking pipes —
Seeing Matthew smoking with the chief,
Minutes before and minutes after
The dunking ceremony
(:I tried to do right. I tried!)
(:Now, Father, hush, we're here)
:Carl's son,
And his arm goes out, recognizing.
:Brother Daniels, I've come to take you for a drive . . .
To the river.
The long-suffering jams his hat on his head
:Father, you hear that? He wants to take you
To the river? Won't that be nice?
But he has been searching not her words,
Nor the poet, but
A remembrance;
The milky intensely blue eyes frown,
Then see the memory.
:You asked me,
The memory asserts authority now,
:How could you know, and I told you I don't know . . .
It's different for every man.

His eyes dance now with the days of two decades ago,
When the boy often touched the time of the old man's living;
When those in the village thought him only pleasantly eccentric,
And blamed him affectionately for being improvident
To his now well-employed children
The saints milked his cows,
Cut his hay,
Stacked it,
While his carefreeness mocked
Their industry and sweat,
With Maori songs; and along the river
He trapped in constant dialogue with elusive fish;
The Saints of Zion loving him full well,
Unconsciously asking him the light and the way,
Envying him, clucking tongues forgivingly
Over the frightfulness of such sloth that dared
Comb abnegation through the beehive of their Mormondom;

Yet innerly knowing he knew secretly
Grandeurs of heaven and earth they
Could only pretend to know
While they righteously worked their days
Honestly
Paid tithes
Honestly
Churched themselves
Honestly
Uttered Sunday platitudes
Honestly
And strove for honest tractors, electricity,
And plumbing, and education;
Acquisitions, all, he never argued with,
But preferred to fish into the cyclic nonsense they are,
Than have.
:It was one day I was hauling straw for your father, down from
Maple field. It was cold that day,
And you were just about knee high to a grasshopper.
Ignoring Sadie's hand, urging him to rise,
To go,
:And you said : I don't know, Brother Daniels,
How does a body go about knowing? And I didn't
Tell you like some others do, to pray and read
The Book of Mormon.
His voice rising, justifying his own form of
Honesty,
His milky intensely blue eyes straining,
Frowning into the Poet's face who
Is remembering that he too was blooded into the village
Life, then.
:Because it's different for every man,
And sometimes when you want to know, you *can't*,
You can't!
That's all there is to it!
He trembles as if
The powerful unseens of orthodox voices
Are claiming otherwise.

:Shhhh, Father . . . now here's your coat . . .
Don't keep him waiting.
:You can't!

Unaware of the coat she has draped over his arm,
Of the Poet's hand guiding him out of the chair,
Of long-suffering holding the door open.
:It's different . . . there's no telling . . .
And the Poet knows there is no telling . . . anything,
For that is why he is back to the old fisherman,
To learn to know, then to tell,
From the spirit of his old and first teacher,
In the glowing dying days;
In hay rack days.
:His arthritis is *so* bad,
Long-suffering's voice a sadness,
A story and a poem
She of patience and no complaints,
Whom no woman in the village ever envied;
She, waiting, knitting the two three four nights
Of his fishing absences,
His announced planlessness
While the hay burned and the unmilked cows
Broke half the fences in town.
:Arthritis this, arthritis that!
Mumbling, staggering,
Critical in his brief return to the world of his long-suffering's
Pitiful narrow-worldness,
She, never having had a vision on a hillside
Or anywhere else,
Never feeling wildly certain of anything
Except a loaf of bread,
A knitted sock.

:The sun was bright as a gold piece,
He says, his joints testing the pathway uncertainly,
:But it was cold that day . . . I tell you . . .
It was awful cold that day . . . and me with a fever
Like a bonfire.
His broken finger joint fumbling over his lips,
He limps and stops, repeating it was different for every man,
But the way he first knew was the night
He lay in a thicket on a New Zealand hillside,
Sick and feverish when
Lo and behold
God and Joseph Smith appeared in a bath of light

:I *saw* them,
He, nearly screaming.
Eyes and lips weeping.
From the porch: Now, Father . . . don't . . . please don't . . .
He turns, walks a jerked speed,
Lips angry now,
Eyes intensely blue searching the gravel path.
:She don't know
They think I'm two shades in the wind;
But they don't know . . . my own house!
But the poet busily deafens the traffic of sadness,
With noises of memory — the sleigh ride day, the load of straw
Among the many loads from maple field,
The snow crusty in the isinglass fields,
Hard and glistening beneath the runners of the long lane roads;
He and the old fisherman buried for warmth in the straw,
Noses dripping and feet yelling numbness,
In the days of dying
When animals seemed the lucky ones,
Fed and warm when humans sometimes weren't:
And the Poet sees the horses foaming in the traces
Snorting and defecating,
Their hooves crunching the hardpacked snow;
And remembering the old fisherman's telling again
Of God and Joseph Smith laying hands upon his fevered head,
Commending him for his faithfulness
In rejecting the chief's request to cohabit
With two of his unmarried daughters,
Hence to plant the seed of Israel in his royal blood;
Then the two personages, glowing brightly as a gold piece,
Commanded the fever from his body,
Bade him rise from the hillside —
:Go forth
And do a mighty work
Among a needful, heathen people;
And if thou are faithful it shall come to pass . . .

But neither in the living nor in the dying years
Did the personages finish their prophecy upon his head,
Leaving him to ask five decades of fishes for the means of his
Salvation.
:I tried,

Limping, clutching the Poet's arm,
:I tried . . . to do my best.
Small compensation since nineteen hundred and twelve
Talking to a river about what living was like,
Convincing elusive fishes of the agony
Of whistling into the graveyard of the villagers' ears
All that they could not know
Of his great knowing . . .

The Poet drives slowly beneath, then into,
The foothills of Pescadero
Seeing a yellow grove of aspens where,
Before his time, a bishop's son
Slew himself herding his father's sheep;
Not listening to the Gabble of where,
In countless fishing holes, the old fisherman
Sought answers to his fate
From fishes.
From hooks to lines to bait to water battles won and lost,
He gabbles.
Finally to Judith, his long-waiting sweetheart,
For whose gospel sake he spurned the barebosomed Maori maids,
He talks;
Of having married her in nineteen hundred and twelve,
Honeymooning at the quarterly gathering of Zion's flock
In Salt Lake City,
There seeing Brother Murdock his New Zealand
Mission President who said,
:Matthew, are you still fishing . . . good! . . .
Hugging the intense villager who
Converted more Maoris than all missionaries combined.
:So busy with real estate and church, I gave it up . . .
Don't let any get away! . . .
. . . But don't forget to love the Lord!
:He was a good man, President Murdock,
Never a better one ever lived.
Crying now, softly,
The big finger crossing under his nose;
For the day after, Judith took sick,
Dying in Salt Lake of appendicitis
Under the prayers of Murdock imploring the Lord
To spare her,

:I come home and started going with Sadie,
He said. But broke off.
:I don't know why I'm a-talking like this,
His eyes coming back with re-interest
As he sees a certain bend in the river,
Beneath Pescadero,
And his spirit lights with memory of a big one,
Landed in Hoover's time,
The very day? (the Poet ponders)
When he, the village constable, forgot to open the polls,
Was off fishing, and the saints had to hoist
A boy through the schoolhouse window.
:Nathan helped me pull him out . . .
Must of weighed six pounds!

Then the narrative of his beginnings,
Flowing as coherently and true as hayrack conversations
In the days of dying—
His father, a trapper named Billings;
Mother a half-breed Indian;
The child orphaned
(:I dunno if they left me or died or what)
And cared for by his mother's people,
Known of, somehow, by the Poet's grandmother who,
Also knowing of Old Gus and Hilda Daniels'
Long childlessness, took him
From the burdened grandparents,
And transported him in a boxwagon
To Bear Lake Valley, keeping him
Alive on mare's milk during the long and delayed journey
From Fort Hall.
Indulged by his foster parents into an idlyllic
River-fishing childhood, permitting him to determine
When or whether to go to school,
And leaving him with reasonable property and money
(As village legacies go) which he used
To perform his three year mission,
Then mismanaged and squandered through neglect
From nineteen hundred and twelve unto this day,
Preferring now, as eight decades ago, to fish
The river every day that the obstructive theys
Will let him,

Crying when they will not.
And through all the days of his dying
Always refusing the complications of family-rearing,
Plying the river for completion of the personages' promises;
But not knowing, the Poet thinks, that he was
Becoming a twentieth-century impossibility,
A wonder of the world that couldn't be,
But was;
Daily returning to the river to secure simplicity;
And though too kind to refuse office and task —
Constable, sexton, gravedigger, butcher —
Too near the magic of idyl to often perform them,
Paying the Saints the inconvenience of his unmilked cows
With messes of fish, and to the bishop too
His tithing — one fish in ten to the Lord.

In the car bumping through pioneer logging trails
Weeded over now, he speaks of recent reform,
Enforced by arthritis and winters too long.
:Been going to church,
He says, like a child learning to swim again.
:Going back now I'm old. But they think I'm
Two shades in the wind and . . .
Choking, bringing the broken joint to his nose,
    . . . :They made me sit down . . . I was telling them
How I came to know . . . fever like a bonfire . . .
Wasn't half through and the bishop told Sadie to make me
Quit.
Because (the Poet thinks) he is the conscience of the village —
The Saints could not bear the chilling pierce of the Maori songs
Cracking the walls of the churchhouse and reminding those
Who have become old with him, that this is his dying year;
Or perhaps, because he announced the chant
As picturing dying suns, they felt
Premonitions of their own Yorick time.
I, the Valley's Poet, stop the machine
That I have accepted as consonant with my century,
And walk in the yellow aspen grove
Where the boy slew himself before my time,
Seeing in the eye of my soul
The Pescadero hills,
The stubble fields, reaped,

And the river, faint and long, below;
Tormenting myself not of dying
But of living in a rocket century.
Knowing the arthritically old man
Trembling in the car
In the final sign of sanity
In this the final year of his dying;
Knowing the *how can anyone know?*
Of our hayrack day gliding over isinglass snow
In maple field is no answer other than
The one he gave, and persisted in.
And now I long for his
Gift of leaving
A way and a time so rich;
To do as he has done;
To be as he has become.
Leaving a river for others to find
For more than they know will be.
Yet who can give such offerings as he,
At the water's edge,
Or offer the gift of self unto its flow?
Who? For eight decades unremitting?
Only he, whose mystery is to be reclaimed in that same innocence
From which, orphaned, he began.
The car starts, moves downhill,
Stung by the lashings of dead willow limbs.
:Be careful, Brother Daniels,
Of the river.
:Tumble in?
Mischief streaking the milky intensely blue eyes,
:O, I 'spect so . . . someday . . . this winter . . . maybe.
Caring not;
For he tried to do right in the days of his living,
Knowing he saw them one rainy night —
God and Joseph Smith.
:I saw them again the other night . . .
Funny thing, they looked a little
Like Judith,
Chuckling, gazing, now pointing the crooked finger to
A certain bend where
He and Nathan pulled a big one
Into shore.

Triad

Stephen
carries secrets he hasn't had time
to decode,
takes his clues from me
as I search for signals myself,
decks his walls with Johnny Cash,
a brass rubbing, a moonshot,
writes a poem: "Get out of my hair, war,"
and in his nightmares is suddenly
grown-up and suddenly irrational
like the grown-up world.

Lorraine
secretes vats of grey matter
in her organic, pulsating room,
creates swirling abstracts
which she sells for pennies,
anxious to be what she is,
she is saved from the cliché
of her Shirley Temple looks
by the butterfly flur
that flits across her face
and curtains her secret self.

Scott
dresses on the move
amid small-craft warnings
of colds and other catastrophes,
smiles and rubs
my lipstick brand,
chooses a coat outgrown last year —
red and blue like Superman's —
walks out alone,
his body enough to shelter him
from rain and other agonies.

Advice

Lift your withered hands and feel
The rush of words push from below.
Lift up your dying hands and write.

Trace the lifted arc of wheel
Pitting itself against the flow
Of earth's slow water in the night.

Force the rigid stone to peel
Back in layers row on row
Its living form against the light.

Coming Apart Together

We exchange in great detail the weather report
We describe our coming decay and dissolution
Your sight has considerably worsened in one eye
Your dentist is into your mouth for five hundred
Your little finger reacts unfavorably to the cold,
and a close friend only four years older died.

I allow as how I'm hiding out from my gynecologist
since he removed certain valuable organs
My neuritis is still making a grand tour
of my body. My skin, it seems,
is deteriorating, my hair congealing,
and a childhood sweetheart died only last month.

And yet, we fall upon each other
in springtime lust just as if we still had
all our teeth, hair, eyesight, and internal organs
just as if we had been created brand new this year
just as if we ourselves had invented
the weather, our bodies, and love itself.

Born Again

As you enter the water unsinning,
I shall repent eight years
Of watching in the dark and loving
Without turning on the light.
I shall shed my old skin,
Remembering you, pink and new,
Unmarked and gifted, my gift
Undeserved.

I have served
My own unmatched desires, a rift
In God's sequence, my blue
Mondays, my bleak Sundays, all kin
To my unshriven blight.
I have loved and been unloving.
To the font I add a cup of tears.
And my own beginning.

Assuagement

I am in the standing position
clothed in a thousand vows
the nails and wedges of law
driven into my shoulders
exposed in my navel
My eyes are aligned and alive
and slit in the erotic mode
I hold my breasts with both hands
in perfect balance
my flexed knees supporting
the blessings of a thousand
matrilinear years
When you look on me, Gelede man,
wear the carved mask and kneel

The Lure

The thread of my life is waxed,
ready to be wrapped on a hook, decorated
with fur and feathers, then flung in a pond.
The fish below — shiners, bluegills, pout —
will watch me floating, dangling helpless.
They will laugh themselves dizzy asking
what fisherman could be sucker enough
to fall for anything phony as that.
They will take turns swirling up through clear
water, at the last moment turn tail
and veer away. The man on the wrong end
of the line will see the ripple and twitch
back his pole. He will curse anxiety and luck,
make another cast. The fish will laugh again,
releasing bubbles of mirth.

                  This will go on
afternoon after afternoon. The sun will beat down
on the fisherman. He will keep casting and missing,
missing and cursing, cursing and — you may wonder
why doesn't he reach down into his tackle box
and try another lure? But the fish are right:
anyone who would cast me out will never come
up with the idea change is in order.

One day the pond will produce the fish who can match
wits with the fisherman: a long pike or heavy trout.
The others will scatter in panic, leaving him
to swim alone, under my shadow. Reflex will turn him,
slowly ascending, opening the dark cave
his jaws make when he holds his breath, gills slack,
tongue flat on the floor. He will feel the hook
tear flesh. His bones will tighten.
The reel will sing to the fisherman whose hands
will remember what to do. I will fall
in love with my captor. His pain will be mine
because he is the only one who ever wanted me.
Together we will rise just as the sun
drops into the kingdom of darkness
where stars refuse to shine.

Confessions of a Disbeliever

When you walk alone wind tries
to tell you something: whispers grass
makes, the semaphore of leaves.

In the dust dark grains rearrange
themselves in patterns you could read
if someone helped you solve the code.

Lines move across the field—wheat
wise enough to survive Pharoah's tomb.
Or across coyote's fur where she sleeps

and waits for the moon when she joins
all her friends to sing the world's secrets
just beyond the edge of town.

Our Town

isn't sure enough of itself
to post a welcome sign.
Winter need never visit us again.
We pride ourselves on our lack
of prejudice—everyone is white.
We can forgive and forget.

My farm forgives the marsh hawk
who flies into the desert each time
she wants to fast, the skunk who tramples
strawberries on his way to corn
leaving a residue of silence,
and the pennies that fall from heaven
and kill the chickens.

We have already forgotten
the woman who jumped from the balcony.
She left her sister's bracelet on the ledge
to prove she was honest. We no longer
remember how the drunk died on his way
to the bank to alter his will.
Each spring we count the lilies
in the fields, although no one knows
just exactly what lilies are.

When the sparrow fell, the sky
left town at midnight.
By morning all the shadows were gone.
I worry about the saxifrage
and each day ask the willow
where are the bees and when will whippoorwills
return to sing?

Porcupine

Two porcupines dead
on the road
within a mile

this morning,
the first I've
seen all season.

No tire scuff
marks where death
came in the night,

guard hairs still
in place, no
streak of blood

nor scattered quills,
everything tidy
like sleeping. No,

it was more
like praying over
folded paws.

*Oh Kaheta, friend of the Paiute, only a starving
man would take your life, giving thanks to four
winds. You never rushed into anything. But we
have forgotten the old gods. We worship diesel,
the sleek sedan. Pray for us, for the wide path
of our intentions paved with stone.*

When It Stopped Singing

Grass, when it stopped singing,
spread silence all over the farm.
We leaned on our pitchforks, looked
up into the eye of a storm.

A cloud looked down, stretched
a dark finger. Wherever it touched
it erased. We ran for the ditch,
lay in it face down, clutched tight

what we found. A sound that began
as a slow freight became
the hooves of all the buffalo
that ever roamed the plains.

I could feel the earth shake.
Buffalo breath tugged at my sleeve.
Above, the hooves pounded over
and over: "Someday the prairie

will be ours again." When it was quiet
I turned to my brother. We climbed
out scared, but alive, looked far
across the land. But the haystack
and all the buffalo were gone.

Sabbatical

Some day I want to take my leave
without a ripple, after the sun turns

sour. Perhaps a night when winds
are calm and the moon turns rain.

You'll be sleeping, of course, but I won't
disturb your rest, just ease through the door,

start walking west. Someone I've known
may feel an emptiness, go to the window

and not know why. Remember the morning
robins stopped singing? Nobody noticed

till after snow. That's how I want to go.
Look for me in the shade of a willow.

Listen hard. Whatever grass says,
it speaks for me.

Children of Owl

When you choose to follow owl
instead of otter, weasel, fox,
you make darkness your friend.
Crow is your enemy, winter
your season, cottonwood
your tree. The old ones tell you
this at twelve when you enter
the *Kiva*, the sweat lodge,
the *Watgurwa*—house of men.
They share ancient secrets,
teach you sacred rites. Silence
is the ultimate virtue,
surprise the weapon you keep
sheathed like talons ready to strike
when stars reveal the slightest
movement below. Death must be swift,
merciful for the unsuspecting
rabbit, the foraging vole: a tuft
of fur, a spot of blood left
beside the perfect cross,
your track in the snow.

KARL C. SANDBERG

Scripture Lesson

Here beginneth the text:

The LORD roars from Zion,
and utters his voice from Jerusalem,
and the heavens and the earth shake.
JOEL 3:16

The roar of the lion, the voice of the fierce lion,
the teeth of the young lions, are broken.
JOB 4:10

And here the interpretation thereof:

There was a time
When the measure of the earth
Was lions.
And the earth was full of lions,
Created by the power of the word,
    the word of a race of mighty men and story tellers
    the words of mighty hunters
    spoken around the stove in winter time
    men lean and strong, each a colossus to my eyes, who
        measured themselves against lions
        in the hills blue with winter.

I thought I knew them and lions
When there was a circus came to Panguitch
    and I saw a man crack his whip,
    saw the lion jump through the hoop,
    saw it do the bidding of the trainer
        and sleep gorged in the cage.
And long I saw thus all lions,
Imagined thus myself a tamer of lions.

Different, I saw, were the men of the hills,
Different the lions,
When Marcus and Merthel came riding down from the
    winter blue mountains,
Rifles in saddle scabbards,
Their pack of hounds following after them,
A mountain lion on the pack horse,
A lion that stretched across the entire kitchen
When they brought it in to show to the invalid grandmother.

Long I looked at this lion,
Did not touch it
    (who would touch a burning bush?)
But ever after thought upon it, and saw him as in life:
    underneath his hide the sinews ran,
    as silently as his feet did
        through the scrub oak and over the ravine,
    crouching to spring
    from the unexpected place.
    And, oh! from out his throat and brain when he roared—
        the sound, immense as all the ancient hills and valleys,
        set the cedars shaking, and the sage hillsides,
        rolling over lines and fences, no one ever knew where
            it would stop.

(From the ranch house near the cedar hills
We sometimes heard the roaring in the night,
And we would have laughed that
Anyone should think to fence it in or out,
    should think to say to the lion
    "Thou shalt not roar now
        for it is not convenient
        for us to hear thee roar"
            or
    "Thou shalt roar just so,
        to me but not to him,
        to us but not to them,
    Thou shalt roar this far and no farther.")

Differently I saw the men who tracked him,
When I too felt the wild cry of blood,
The cry to go with them,
Endlessly with horse and baying dogs
    across day and night,
    not resting, fascinated,
    drawn on to hear the mortal snarling, to see his claws
    ripping the hounds, when he was brought to bay,
    to see his eyes flash,
    at that one moment,
    defiance of men and hounds and all beyond.

Yes, how different then
    for my eyes was the lion that jumped
Through the hoop
At the bidding of the trainer,
How different the world
    when emptied of lions
Except those that
    sleep gorged in a cage.

Autumn

On the coolness of the nights an edge,
The crickets have begun to send a different call,
On the highest slopes the fluttering aspen leaves have turned.
Shoulders slump, feet shuffle more than step.

Seed has been cast,
Has grown to what it will,
Full or half or stunted in entangling grass,
No matter. The growing time is done.
Hands tremble. Small, familiar ways become estranged.
Eyes will sometimes look away
Without looking.

A voice expected full comes thin.
Morning ice will form transparent on the ponds,
Geese will fly, the earth wind down.
"Wilson came to me last night.
He said I'm almost there."
Sadness and anticipation enter in.

Night Watch

No, I think you do not hear aright.
The wind, it does not make a moan,
Or any personal lament.
It is but the passing
Of this January night
Over miles and miles of Pleistocene stone.
No, you should not lend the cold a mind,
And in the dark is no intent
Of malice, harm, or slight,
Nor will, of course, that is properly its own —
But let us cease our prattle
And let this gaunt Sanpete County farmer
Die alone.

Red Buttes in Navaho Country

I

The hunter among the Navahos, they say,
Does not pursue the deer. He waits,
And since all things converge
Along fine but sometimes visible lines,
He draws the deer to him,
And slaying the deer, he thanks it,
That it has let itself be slain.

II

This land will yet elude my eyes.
I contemplate these buttes,
And see that years in tedious thousands
Swallow up my power to imagize or grasp.
Still, it is visible that rain has fallen,
Wind has hurled sand against the rock,
Forms have emerged, receptacles of species
That appeared and disappeared as specks
Between Alpha and Omega indifferent.
I contemplate these buttes,
A speck among the specks.

I point this out to those I pitied for their poverty,
So poor of thought and language
That in the very moment they opined
A godless and indifferent nature,
They conjured up a savant lady
With hair upon her chest,
Who never ceased intending something
And thus got up on her hind legs
And walked around. Why put out our eyes
With the language of illusion?

This is a solitary land.
Let the language be precise and calipered,
I said, not overstepping by a hair
The line of what is seen.
(Or else agree eviction papers
Still have not been served
On the teeming goddess in the test tube.
Give at least the homage of a lucid eye to life, to death.

III

In afternoon, the hillside shadows in the ledges move,
Forming as a thought within the mind.
What is visible is what has gone
And still surrounds.
Was it Jonah who was right,
Who could not go where God was not,
Finding everywhere in everything
The mirror of something else?

I watch within and see myself a seer
Where these same buttes are part of me,
And I within an atom's world
Where twenty billion revolutions
Are but a day, a mayfly life,
Which by thought I come to see
From the turning of a larger sphere.

I am the water and the sand,
I the stone, and I the wind,
I am a parcel of the privileged light
That is and sees the layers stripped away
And hews the form of what is left,
In the silence of the hunter,
In the stillness of the buttes,
Dark red in the land of the Navahos.

LEWIS HORNE

21st Birthday

The small child is never far away
Though you're adult now with an eye
Miranda-bright and a groundling giggle
For the quirks and funnies we — your parents — find
Too daily for amusement in this world.
The land of dragons, Aslan and the White Witch,
The creatures of Oz bits-and-pieced together —
All cross still with a racy life
Too natural to marvel your mind.

Words come from your tongue *vivace*,
Borne *prestissimo* out of total recall.
It's not my fancy only that finds in your face
Today — an adult, yes — the same Christmas-tinsel
Dazzle and love of Santa Claus, still the child
As you sit across the restaurant table from me.
A "daddy-daughter" thing, your mother away.
What shall I say? What can I tell you
But you're twice-distilled for beauty.

Driving my Daughter to Moose Jaw
For her Patriarchal Blessing

Driving south, we watch the snow across
The fields churn in wind like chaff. The way
It feathers the road, we think of cold stretched high
And pegged as though there's nothing it divides
With itself, no compromise it makes. The fields
Are frozen hard enough to clink and clank
Beneath a hammer. The car's savannah warm
And coats are off. Her head pillowed on
The armrest, our daughter sleeps through early morning.
The bare sky is hanging without form.

From Saskatoon to Moose Jaw, snow cleared
By wind, the fields turn dark, while farther sand
For safety darkens the road curving into
The Qu' Appelle Valley and out. Huts barnacle
The white surface, homes for ice-fishers.
Across the ice and fields, across the sky,
Burrowed in silence — where is intent?
The fishermen are hidden. Scarcely a car
Hails the road. Goals are hidden. Warmth
In the car for us is heater, yes, and spirit —

What we're intent upon. Our daughter wakes.
We find, new in a field to the edge of the city,
The Moose Jaw Mormon chapel, our coldland harbor.
She has prepared, our daughter, for her blessing,
A caution and a comfort and a promise,
From a patriarch called of . . . Who by his power . . . A part
Of intent, her contract for more chilling seasons
And the tantrums of more distant borders.
Little by little we see her go. It's our
Intent. How perfectly serene the cold.

EUGENE ENGLAND

My Kinsman

*If we live in our holy religion and let the spirit reign, it will not
become dull and stupid, but as the body approaches dissolution the
spirit takes a firmer hold on that enduring substance behind the
veil. . . .*

— BRIGHAM YOUNG

My father's flesh appears the same,
Brown clay so burned by summers
In the wheat that still the hat line
Shows lighter into the failing hair.

But more than half the third finger
On the left is gone, the fourth clipped
By the same saw, and crooked just right
To hook the twine for tying sacks.

And on the right two toes removed
(Years later) against the constant pain
From being crushed by the big roan
As she stepped and turned to leave the stall.

A wedge of bone, ploughed from the skull
When the derrick fork pinned him to the stack.
The muscles slack, the teeth reduced —
The body's edges worn away.

The tabernacle shrinks and sinks
Toward the earth, and still the face
Juts toward the east, the hands grasp the wheel
As they did the morning I was eight:

We drove from town just as the sun
Squinted down Left Fork into our eyes.
We stopped the truck and crossed the swale
To the highest ridge on the lower field —

The stalks still green, the heads just formed,
Beards now turning silver-tan,
Still and moist in the windless dawn,
Closing calmly as we walked the rows.

Plucking random heads, we counted and chewed
The milky kernels. And then he knelt,
Still grasping the wheat, in fierce repose.
I stood and watched his face. He said:

"Thou are the Prince who holds my heart
And gives my body power to make.
The fruit is thine: this wheat, this boy;
Protect the yield that we may live!"

And fear thrilled me on that hushed ground,
So that I grew beyond the wheat
And watched my father take his hold
On what endures behind the veil.

The Temenos

This neutral room, enclosed and left to books
Subdues the terror that my thought regains.
These myths I read diffuse it — paradox
Pervades to blunt the evil that remains:

Brusque summer sky — blurred wind and sun composed
The air, and dark was all we waited for,
Threshing the grain from dust and straw. We paused
Before the cool point of the evening star.

With horses fed, relaxing stiffened eyes
And skin, I moved down to the sheltered creek —
And found the snake, total in coiled daze,
Beneath the calming leaves. My mind seeks back
To try again the old repulse, to think
That lifted circle on the darkening bank.

Sunrise on Christmas

Looking up the glacial valley of the Weber
Into the high Uintahs, past fading trails
Where Bannock and Shoshoni summered into Colorado,
I see light grow out above the southeast ridge.
    Ah, it is the day returning,
        Pale upon my face;
    It is the ancient figure of my hope.

Three days ago, with a mind of winter, I marked
Again the edge of the dead lodgepole's first shadow
On the aspen log, where other marks in shortening steps
Converged to this mark, repeated at the dark solstice.
    Ai-ya! It is the sun's death
        And cold upon my breath;
    It is the stillness of the turning point.

Now where I kneel to see the shadow of the rising fire
The first rays glitter around distant spruces
But fix the shadow back a tiny step,
Returning to the south of earlier ones.
    My God, it is the sun returning,
        Burning on my face.
    It is the April blood upon my tongue.

Cri du Chat

*The most remarkable feature of the "Cri du Chat" syndrome
is the one for which it is named: the shrill and
plaintive nature of the infant's cry, unmistakably
calling to mind the mewing of a kitten.*
— JEAN DE GROUCHY, Clinical Atlas of Human Chromosomes

How could a cat's cry be the voice of God?
Yet he will speak there, swift, inerrant, awed
Perhaps by his own sorrow for this child
Who mews at birth. The seamless sound comes wild
To the ears of parents. They recoil, stilled
With fear. Sometimes they dream that they had killed
It from the womb, had warned themselves with cold
Knowledge through amniocentesis, boldly
Flushed away the foetus, so that the wide-
Set eyes and moon-wide face had never cried
This way. But they had not: They find God's word
Not in some pure, intending force that stirred
The dark tangle of chromosomes and cut
Merely one tip of number five so that
The child lives on, losing the cry, but void
Of language, sense, response, its features called
Monstrous. It seems, to them, God speaks in dreams
Of their responsibilities.

Pilgrims

I. *Oncorhynchus tschawytscha*

Honorable dead Chinook, tyee, King,
You heaved one hundred pounds up the Yukon
To deposit milt on her eggs drifting
In the silt of the graveled hollow you made
With your thinning head, your jaw hooked over
Itself, your throat closed so you would not stop
And return to the sea to eat. Your rich, red flesh
That leaped all falls kept you alive and now
Dissolves into the stream that feeds your young.

II. *Rangifer caribou*

The slipping tendons click over bones in your feet
When you move—a quarter ton. You belch a grunt
And the calves bawl, all along the line
That streams thousands a thousand miles
From this woodland bay north to the tundra,
Where lichens grow, and the sedges—
Except for the hundreds who starved or broke
Through the ice, the calf you left for the wolves,
And you, now in the cross hairs.

III. *Archilochus colubris*

Returning to nest, your body tilts until
Your blood-gem throat leads across the Gulf.
Your wings stroke down, then turn full over
To stroke up as strong—fifty per second.
Five hundred miles costs one tenth of you.
You feel magnetic current from the poles;
You sense the turning earth; your eye measures
The changing angle, sun against dark sea,
To guide you home.

Faith

Sacramental hours
cross this chapel of infinity
where the arch of the brain dreams horror.
And no one comes.
Within the waiting shadows
the silence says wait:
the darkness is a piece of a piece
in the rapture of even being.
But no one comes.

Manti Temple

A faceless stone stands above my valley,
pushing the broad seasons before it into
millennia of green light. And the sky
surrounds the stone confession of courage in
an intercourse of blue voices unscarred
by preposterous sky-foam of star-crossed man.
The stone is a stark sail for our eye,
set upon a sea of its own, leading
our washed feet and naked souls upon
the bread-strewn waters of our faith,
where are carved cherrystones into stars.

My Children on the Beach at Del Mar

These are fragments of myself
playing at being fragments of myself
and they will become fragmented themselves
as like me they become themselves.

But then all things explode,
nothing is, all things become,
not merely changing but expanding
and not merely growing, progressing, but exploding.

So my children, fragments
of a fragment fragmented forever,
playing pieces of a creation,
Creation playing with pieces.

So the born idea
that ought to have a life of its own
but breaks into many voices,
tones, phones, particles.

So the single decision
used to define a morality
making courses of action, destinies,
cosmic avalanches of effect.

So the quick hand,
imagination in a linguistic accident,
traveling from eye to mind
from mind to eye interminably.

All is not nothing but pieces,
pieces and process, a wave
breaking into many waves
and breaking again at my feet.

All going, all gone, all lost,
what was begun unique
becomes duplicity, trinity, variegate, infinite:
thus genesis is very soon apocalyptic

with time the maker and the villain.
My God the sun a hole
a way out we turn it greys
you've closed it you've closed the way out!

Creation

God may have his presence
in silence only,
made so that a man
may have space and time
to make himself himself.
Whatever is is lost—
but the unmade silences
teach hope, and possibility,
and all the virtues
God gave men
to make gods of themselves.
Whatever is made
belongs to God.
But wherever silence is
man steps in
and becomes,
encounters time
and unmade space,
working in a way
no other one
has ever wrought.
And what he makes of silence
becomes, like God,
himself.

RONALD WILCOX

Multiplicity

Multiplicity 1

There has been one and one only perfect moment
when the awful machinations of chance completely and smoothly meshed,
    each part moving in single precision,
when the intricate multiplicity of myriad circumstance,
    warm as shimmering hints of first life in the womb of our mother sea,
was unified in peace and simplicity easily as the hidden logic of healing,
moved in that moment beyond even mercy, almost to comprehension,
and the memory of God being born that day split infinity to forever
    be recorded in all living things,
                                among whom man, remember, is only one,
and this holy inclination, irretrievably barbed within the inmost core
    of the gene and seed of each cell of our being,
        is unequivocal as the sea's unfathomed geometry
which patterned impulse into pulse as life first stirred.

Multiplicity 2

There is an unnamed mesa in northwest New Mexico
eroded by the holy wind into a form as pure as an abandoned cathedral.
If you could climb to the top just before morning,
you might find the oldest living Navajo man, the patriarch Narbona,
who more than a hundred years before this day hid himself forever
    within the enigma of the cliffs of his youth,
sitting hunched over his holy campfire, facing the eastern indistinct horizon,
awaiting the daily resurrection of his undying sungod,
muttering his ancient Athapascan incantations, whose meaning only he remembers,
in order that morning will send death this day winging like a golden arrow
    through his dry vitals
to snuff the last spark of life he feels glowing still amid his dusty bowels
whose ashes stir like the restless colorless embers which the wind disturbs
    before him,
and if you could stand exactly southeast of his wrinkling squint,
you might perceive in his brief and milky upward glance

reflections of the careless scatterings of the last stars in the nighttime
     morning sky,
and in the movement of his eyes you could follow the subtle convolutions
     of his mind
as it etched upon the unrolling scroll of man's most ancient unfaded manuscript
     irrevocable lines between the stars,
lines invisible yet palpable, mathematically exact as a navigator's projection,
and with the low moon over his shoulder, like a dull lamp whose amber glow
     lulls as it dies,
he would read a secret language spelled in those crisscross tangents,
for the calligraphy of his prophecy is written in flickering code,
     the silent telegraphy of the wireless ether;
the clear and piercing air of the silvered desert is to him sharper than
     firewater,
more intoxicant than the first long draught of chilled pure alcohol of water
     distilled in the crystal of a mountain spring,
and drunken in deep inhalation, his eyelids would droop and flutter;
he would see in this moment of drowse an unbidden instant's mirage,
     hovering low as a smoke signal,
an inexplicable puff of something never seen before
                    at the edge of that vast and faceless distance,
but shot through with fear, he would suddenly start awake,
          shake himself loose of his vision,
forget forever the unbearable moment of knowing,
for he would have seen clear meanings advancing,
flashing like a black thundercloud crackling with sudden comprehensions,
electric with threats of the consequences of unspeakable possibilities,
the naked face of unforgivable sin, knowledge of the final pith of things,
and trembling uncontrollably, he would draw his humanity up over his eyes
          like a patterned blanket and hide, blindly patient,
awaiting the warm morning farewell and all-reaching embrace of Death,
     his last fellow savage,
who would welcome him home as a friend returning from a long trek
     through pathless lands, the endless timbered slopes of his life;
then you may see the long shadows of sunrise reach for him
     through the sparse, hushed grass at the mesa's rim,
and up from the chanting cactus
                              locusts would rise like angels
and fly with his soul in their wingtips.

Multiplicity 3

On October 13, 1161 A.D., Awkwahtawn, the Huron Iroquois, blazed with his
    death song —
                        Chen Chen CHEE-kawn-wah
wailed through his blistered lips,
bubbled forth from his heart's core like boiling oil,
congealed in the wavering air like blood from his open wounds —
    Chen Chen CHEE-kawn-wah!
His enemies, the Seneca Iroquois, had impaled Awkwahtawn for seven days —
    slow roast on a spit;
how they had mumbled over his hovering in awe of his unflinching smile,
    his clear, sweet song —
                        Chen Chen CHEE-kawn-wah!
Now he sang in their savage dance as added branches burst and split
    with buds of fire, as in spring,
consumed his soul with leaves of flame, as in autumn.
. . . sparks whirled like stars,
and shedding his flesh in layers, as he would winter's weathered deerskins
    in the heat of a sudden spring sun,
his pure spirit was ringing clear as a cool waterfall rilling in ferned pools
    round stumps where his feet once were —
                        Chen Chen CHEE-kawn-wah!
Visions, whispering cold as winds amidst the pine,
fell lightly as snow past the tatters of his face, over his raked flanks,
    and downward until the flames themselves seemed frozen numb.
Awkwahtawn was dimly aware of lumps of ice bluntly nudging at his legs —
    Chen Chen CHEE-kawn-wah!
His nerves, ever hard and sharp as flints in his skin,
were finally dulled against those cold, vague stalagmites,
and far above dying Awkwahtawn a hovering eagle startled at his final cry
    and soared toward the sun, calling —
                        Chen Chen CHEE-kawn-wah!

Multiplicity 4

The thought of his own death stirred in the brain of Mr.
John Edward Sheisty, 3327 Erstwhile Street, Los Angeles, Calif.,
once in the fall of 1947,
but he quickly forgot it, made believe, in fact, it hadn't happened.
The moment lasted exactly one millimeter of the movement of the pendulum moon

over San Fernando Valley:
time hung shocked in that moment of no movement, like
    (1) an October gourd
    (2) the last throb of the stopped heart
    (3) the clam-like glob of the insensate brain
        just before catching on to a joke
    (4) the unspoken plea when you're losing the game
        ("For gosh sakes, time out!")
    (5) a moment of pause between heaves of morning nausea;
in other words,
it lasted approximately as long as $.3^3$ times the first jerk
    of the shuddered spasm of the not quite immaculate conception
of the all but engendered John Edward Sheisty (affectionately nicknamed
    "Shy Jack" by his buddies on the high school track team in 1927
solely because of a painful reticence on his part in regard to fornication,
    the fourth most popular activity of the student body,
a nickname which stuck and which most conscientiously in all modesty
    he had had printed in parentheses upon calling cards
        JOHN EDWARD (SHY JACK) SHEISTY
of his small real estate business, a growing concern in the valley
    of the San Fernando at the time,
a moderate supply of the which his wife would conscientiously slip
    like a packet of ammunition
into the breast pocket of his fresh white shirt each morning,
    including Sunday);
                but it never happened again,
not even on the day he died,
lullabied by anesthetics between hygienic white sheets of a sterilized
    hospital bed.
(It seems his nurse tiptoed his soul painlessly away
    in a shining aluminum bedpan
toward a reward of 99 and 44/100% pure oblivion,
an event recorded quite properly in history and eternal pity
    by the Los Angeles Times obit section sometime in spring, 1948.)

Multiplicity 5

Rock on the moon and noon rock glinting beneath a stream. Rock.
Gleam of rock, sea-sown and free, green-blue, miles deep.   Rock.
Wayward rock, sun-powdered and sand-encrusted,
    vague unshaven faces of rock.

                          Shaled waves of prairies,
brushed rock set hard and skimming
   in mirages.
Rocks,
breaking down sides of cliffs, caught in crags, hot, weltering visions.
Rocks like dead eyes, set stones in skulls of white rock.
Rock of the earth, never seen, never known, heart of rock,
   beneath the green shade. Rock.
Rock on rock on rock.
Dull and delving rock and cold volcanoes, cool obsidian mirrors,
   clear black rock like liquid unmoving.
Quicksilver stars.
Rocks, time-shattered, split uneven into shards of razors, wind-sanded.
Rainbow rock, slippery scars of oily sun. Rock.
Deep wounds of red rock, cut rock, crawling with things under,
   stinking wet rock.
Virtual, flickering, floating in the tube, gray TV,
   rock like smoke or milk in water, rock-images on the moon.
Slow sea-wind over the shore spraying rocks, smell of moss and weed.
Sandcrabs playing at rock, all crustacean, unexplained,
   moving in glue, untoward.
Sea-slime swimming and weaving amid undersea pillars of sun, spots of rock,
   pied rush of currents and leanings.
Rocks careening like processes of thought, mad as cathodes on the moon,
   the shattered lens of the sea, the glass earth hung in space,
                                   flung
   like a round blue rock through a great black window.

Multiplicity 6

Sing the vision of intelligence:
of feeling beings, being touched, touched by, touching their environment,
being in and surrounding, surrounded by and part of, never harming
   the roiling patterns of their Creator.
These Great Whales.
See them turn in splendid wellings of whitespray and sun,
   great folding hands painting in blue oils sea and sky.
Catch them at the edge of breaking glass waves,
   surfacing in the skim of reflecting eyes,
      breathing in consistencies of waking days,
crying to their own through translucencies of sound and skin.

Follow them through deep ocean currents, sentience illimited,
echoing organ sounds within this emerald cathedral, the sea,
where all lives are ceremonies and each movement bends in dependency,
in processions of fish and solemn masses, communions of appetite,
    subsumed in fathoms, the earth like a crystalline grail,
for in themselves they eat of their symbols, themselves,
    believing all pain has meaning and an end.

Multiplicity 7

They say they sang "Fair Mary Kelly, my girl, my love," as they marched
    blue as the Fourth of July against a green hill in Georgia
        in dust and rows of regulars and recruits,
a song made up out of his own head by 1st Lt. John Anderson, Union Army,
    lean and yankee in the trust of his own strength in the bosom of God,
sang out his love who lived up the road as far as Kentucky is:
    soon the blue troops, whistling in tune the tune in his head;
    soon the gray bullets, whistling the tune out of his head.
Go up the road, at this moment, far away in Kentucky.
Watch "Fair Mary Kelly," with his love like a song in her sides,
    battering her way inward, far off the road, running away
        to a place she knows of, branches scratching at her breasts,
white dress tattered like pale leaves.
Pad with her heavily through this thick pine shade, moss and thicket,
    one two one two one two through trees one two.
Feel her breathe.
See her black eyes shine. Deer, darting.
Call her, as he did, "gallant" Mary Kelly, holding her belly in both hands,
    for all she cares,
for you may marvel at her two bare feet
    moving forward one two one two over a trail hardly there.
See through her wild black hair halfway in her eyes.
"What shall I name him?"
One two, running now.
"John's a good name. Jesus loved him."
Sing, oh, where will Mary Kelly lie? So fair.
    In his bosom. In his deep bosom.
Wake in your heart the moistness of her love.
With her, clutch at your lungs, stiffen your spine,
    arch your back against the great trunk of a tree,
        fallen, secretly, in this deep green forest hollow.

Moan your love, grieving and grave.
Believe in the deep shade of trees and grass,
    and in the shade of its secrecy.
Pull the white dress up past the white pelvis.
Heave, with her, with all your heart, the deep hurt of her love.
Spread the skeleton buried in her hips.
Push out with weeping ease the promise made in a deep night
    in a chill October bed last year
where John, my John, oh, God, my Father, hear my cries in this wilderness,
    and, if you find heart enough, hang in her eyes,
        suddenly still in spasm, in a black hawk hovering far overhead,
for now you are more than woman and man and God made one in union,
    you are, in this thrust-forth of flesh, life!
A tiny steaming throb in the grass, suddenly wounding the world.
For your loins and your soul and hers are the same.
One long last wrench and heave, unbearable, after.
Her heart, and yours, lies red and splashed in the grass.
Moan in this silent and empty place where beats no sound save the wind
    in a far echo over the trees.
Sobbing
against this great silent fallen tree hidden miles from her home in town,
far from those lies of the news of her yankee lover when John left home
    last year for the north, for the war far away in Georgia,
        not good gray but a cursed blue, they say,
sobbing, ease now carefully arched hips down,
    ease the stretch of your thighs,
        outraged, down,
into cool moist grass under white buttocks.
Now, reach with the wonder of your love to your heart and wait for a wail.
No sound.
Pick him up.
The world balanced in the blackness of space, the held moment of man,
    here in your hands.
Life in his lungs with your hands.
Hear, for the very first time
    the very first cry and tiny air and know your world moves
in the fathomless vastness of the gaze of God in a hawk far overhead,
    hovering, held in the wind, like a held breath.
John, still,
though you never knew,
who went down on the 4th of July to a green battle in Georgia,
    lying red in the grass,

splashed against the side of a hill, in a blue uniform.
A new John, dutifully found by searchers from town in the goodness of time
    and July 4, 1864.
You'll hang in a locket on his neck,
    though you'll never know,
your fading tintype face encased in the silver lace locket inscribed,
    "My mother, Mary Kelly Anderson, called fair.
        Died in my childbirth, lived in my heart."
For ninety-seven years, three polygamous wives, twenty-seven children
    living and dead, one hundred thirty-two grandsons and daughters,
        from them great-families, living thoroughly,
a man, John,
on a globe held blue and suspended in your love,
    birthed on a bright July day in a secret hollow only you knew.
Your heart you squeezed through your thighs, Mary Kelly,
    in a summer afternoon deep as Kentucky.

A Skeleton's Reappraisal

The objective eye must see itself first,
last longer than the mirror it peers out of.
The steady voice must never tremor longer
than low tones in the ozones of reason.
Yet, perception lingers in the nostrils,
deceives the sensual man remembering clearly
blue air and summer days that never were.
The touch of her skin, smooth as new parchment,
cools through the years; her lovely name is
written in faint odors of invisible lemon.
Decipher the code of stones dotting old graves,
semaphores of lovers entwining in the weeds.
Disentangle your past from what it was with hers:
you will know your own nerves spun into soft
webs underground, your widening smile, dusted
with her love, lying through the teeth of time.

ELOUISE BELL

Psalm for a Saturday Night

Bring forth thy Sabbath, O Lord,
    For I am ready.

I have anointed my head with jubilation
    Pressed from thy ripest blessings.
My soul has been washed in thy raining grace,
    And I am clean and shining.
O deliver thy Sabbath, for I await!

I have clothed me in a garment of repentance;
    The ragged sins of this week have I cast off.
My hair is perfumed with the unguent of forgiving:
    There remains no burr or tangle to snarl the sweep of love.
O sanctify thy Sabbath, and let its mantle fall about me!

I have adorned my hand with jewels of compassion.
    My feet are shod with eagerness for thy service.
Here in the pulsing darkness I bate my breath
    And urge the stars on in their passage.

Bring forth thy Day, O Lord,
    For thy servant waits.

"This Do in Remembrance of Me"

Blinking out into the April brightness
One Sabbath after church,
I heard a Saint expound to a politely listening friend,
"With us, the sacrament is just a symbol."

"Just a symbol."
All the sunlong day and starlong night
Those slippery words shadowed me.

True enough: the bread but bread.
Yet the body offered
Up was real,
Its shattered nerves most verifiable
As pain spiked along the net.

Right enough: the water nothing more.
But the shed blood pulsed power-poor,
Streamed swift, then slow, to dry and cake
Down racked arms and flanks.

How pallid the bread when pale the memory.
Yet sweet the nourishment when we his Spirit summon
By rich remembering.

Every symbol has two halves.
But to us falls the matching.
What match we, then, in sacramental token?
What fit we to the water, and the bread?

ROBERT A. REES

Fishers

(fishing with my son on the Upper Weber)

In the last days of summer
we walk through tall grass
to the river
long before the sun spills
over the mountains.
We cast into morning air.
He flits like a water skeeter,
impatient for the taut nudge, the sudden pull.
"Be still," I say, "you'll scare the fish."

> *the river rolls over the rocks,*
> *tumbling mauve and ochre stones*

But still he stalks the fish,
an ancient angler
crouching in wet grass.
"Where are all the fish?" he asks.
"Here, where the current slides away;
there, by that big rock."

> *there, where the shards of morning*
> *break deep on stippled stones,*
> *where clouds wash over wild and watery weeds*

Shadows recede against the mountains.
He asks, "Where do fish come from?"
"Some have lived here for many years;
others are planted each spring
by the hatchery."

> *they swim from secret pools in the sky,*
> *from starry rivers among the spheres, like birds*
> *that fly through seas on fluent wings*

"Have there always been fish?"
"As long as anyone remembers,
long before your grandfather and your great-grandfather,
long before the Indians were here."

> *ancient fish swim down the headwaters of time,*
> *from old lakes deep as skies, where*
> *Indians wait for rain*
> *on a seamless shore*

Still the fish ignore our hooks
and still he wonders,
"What do fish bite?
What do they like to eat?"
"Sometimes corn or salmon eggs;
night crawlers are usually best,
although they love insects."

> *insects with frail iridescent wings*
> *swim in the wind — mayflies and moths,*
> *bumblebees and beeflies, golden-eyed lacewings*
> *and black-winged damselflies dance before*
> *shifting and sliding rainbows*

"What kinds of fishes are there?"
"Mostly trout here — rainbows and a
few browns. Over in the lake there
are bluegill and perch."

> *sturgeon old as stone,*
> *walleyed pike and yellow perch,*
> *black bass, mackerel, and blue pickerel,*
> *brown trout, rainbow trout, and silver salmon*
> *glide and turn in the crystal night,*
> *their scales catching slanted sun*

"Did you use to go fishing with Grandad?"
"When I was a boy, we'd get up
at three in the morning
and drive over Mt. Hood
to the Deschutes River where we'd
catch trout as big as your arm."
"Who's best, you or Grandad?"
"Grandad's pretty good.
He can catch fish where no one else can."

our ship sails over the mountain toward the
dawn where, in the morning mist, deer
run before us as in a dream;
at the river my father watches the wind and the
water for signs I cannot discern, and suddenly a
giant trout jumps into the air to greet us,
his mottled body silvers the sun
before my startled eyes

"But the greatest fisher of all
lived a long, long time ago. They called him
the Fisher King, and the fish of all the
waters listened for his voice, and when
he called them or when he sang his song,
they came right up to him."
He arches his eyebrow: "Really?
That's just a story, isn't it, Dad?"
"Maybe, maybe not."

fish leap before him as he walks
on the waves, and whales praise him
from the great green sea;
he casts his net into the brine and
heaves it brimming into the boat,
and at the psalming of his voice,
the fish dance joyfully about his feet

"Dad! Look! I've got a bite!"
His pole arches against the sun
and dips into the river.
"Hold him! Reel in, reel in!
That's it, don't lose him! Steady now."
The stippled trout flops
wildly at his feet;
he watches it with wonder.

When the sun reaches its zenith
my son and I turn from the river and
walk toward the mountain
through summer air filled
with incense of sage.
His fish in one hand, he reaches up
and puts his other in mine.
"Thanks for taking me fishing, Dad," he says,
"I love you."
And a fish leaps in my breast

> *and into the sky, arching over*
> *all streams and all seas,*
> *a rainbow over the broken world*

Somewhere near Palmyra

"The glory of the City was the temple of the sun."
— WILL DURANT

He saw something that morning
deep among the delicate leaves
burning against the Eastern sky—

    The sun and suns,
    radiance enfolded
    in oak and elm

    visages of light
    luminous as seer stones
    rinsing the still grasses

    personages of fire,
    jasper and carnelian,
    dispersing the morning dew:

    images that bore him
    through dark of night,
    terror of loneliness,
    blood of betrayal,
    the ache of small graves,
    to death from the prison window
    where, wings collapsing
    through the summer air,
    he fell—

And I know, kneeling
among the secret trees
this winter morning
where no birdsong rings
among the barren bush
and no leaves spring green,
where darkness thickens and gathers
among the withered weeds
and my tongue is a fish
under the river's roof,
that I too see what he saw —

    sun, light, fire —

images of glory
flashing through the morning mist.

Gilead

The sugar maple burns
against the sky,
flowering among sage and juniper,
cedar and pine,
as if it alone drank summer sun,
mirroring in final flame
that golden circumstance.
Its fire is the heart
of the mountain that lights
the trees of all the wood:

the florescent tree
at the edge of Eden
where cherubim still circle;

the incandescent bush
where Moses trembled
when the Word bound his bones;

Lehi's luminous tree,
whose fruit divide the night
like ripe moons;

the fresh-cut evergreen,
its colored candles
swaddling starlight;

and the broken branch
where the light was nailed,
and all the leaves turned red;

the golden bough of Byzantium,
among whose fine hammered leaves
the holy birds still sing;

and, at the end, the timeless tree
reflected in the river,
its twelve fruit the balm of nations —

and at once all the trees of the field
clap their hands and rejoice,
sending their roots along the stream,
their foliage ever green
against the dying year.

October 9, 1846

Listless as game birds
that moult to signal another change
of season, the last saints straggled
to the river bottoms. They'd seen
the temple finished, seen the sacred
and the profaning, and were easy enough

then to flush: the sick who waited
to bury their dead, the poor waiting
on spring or goods from the Twelve.

At noon, children saw the men kneel again.
Reading well the white silence of women's
faces, they crept like Indians through
the brush, foot exactly in front of foot,
and found a feather or two, some empty
snail shells.

A sudden whir, a throaty trill, the swell
of speckled wings: and the dry beds filled
with food. The quail came, strutting
the camp, tracks faint as scattered chaff.
The pear-shaped birds did not flatten
shy and wild in the grass. Crested heads
pivoted from child to child who picked
them, eyes wide at the bloodbeat of such
feathered fruit.

No gun was needed to feed these six hundred
destitute. Six times the birds circled
the camp, six times landed. At each rising
the flock increased, and at the seventh
swell, the mottled augury took leave
     that saints might praises sing
        while making way to the Great Salt Lake.

For Linda

I. The Viewing

If only there were daisies here in tin cans.
These flowers are too nice: ivory-tongued anthurium,
gladiola mouths holding their long, red O's
while Sister Smith whispers, "Aren't the roses
something? They'll open at the cemetery."
And she goes on: both legs broken, neck snapped,
steering wheel right through your ribs.

The mortician had left them alone, she says.
He'd handled a Mormon funeral before, in Detroit.
And your spirit hovered near the three old women
called to dress you. They felt it

while they stretched garment strings, pulled
white nylons over legs pieced together in plastic
bags. What lifting to fit you into that white
dress, to tie the apron just right. They've patted
you into place, tidy as the bread you daily baked.

The sister smooths the robe, fluffs the bow.
How she must have worked, her fingers coaxing
yours to an attitude of rest. Tomorrow's time
enough for the just to rise; today you're ready
for viewing.

2. The Services

The meetinghouse fills. Did you know every Jack-
Mormon in Michigan? The bishop tells us you never
uttered a cross word — you could scold him so
he should know the mortician drained blood yesterday.
Already, bigger than life is better than life.

The family's here (all but the minister-father
who preached all things pure to the pure in heart
and abused his daughters). Your brother, the first
Mormon among them, bows his head. His wife
never accepted such unrestraint, but she cries.

Even your coming into the church was unrestrained.
So evidently pregnant the elders thought you
properly married. And you said yes, the divorce
final, the new marriage made, when your brother
flew in to baptize you. A year later the stake
president called for a long interview.
Baptized as though bearing the name of the man
in your home and now wanting to go to the temple.

You called your brother then to explain it all.
How could his wife know that sins, though scarlet,
would be white as snow? Whiter even than the putty
of your face. The freckles never showed so before.

And then all those babies. Eleven times, yeasty
as the loaves of bread you kneaded. Seven sons
from such risings, the newest seven months old.

This is not moderate, your going so.

3. *The Dedication*

We do not have enough processional flags.
More people drive to the township cemetery
than are buried there. The maples are still yellow,
but everyone says snow is in the air.

A Mormon can dedicate a grave in less than three
minutes and leave you to loose soil. I'll come back
tonight and gather the fat roseblanket, all these
wreaths. But I will not bring daisies. The maples
will be enough. And the wind that testifies a presence
by the space it leaves when passing through.

Oleander

"... if a male child unfortunately dies
... we don't take gruel for a year
And if we fail to kill a daughter,
again we skip a meal a day in sorrow,
and thus also save some money for her marriage."
    ANNAMAYAKKAL OF SINGARASPURAM,
    India Today, *June 15, 1986*

The blood has not yet clotted
the cloth between her thin legs
when the woman in the thatched hut
begins stripping oleander stems.

Mashing a few berries,
she dips her smallest finger
into the milky paste,
then gives it
to the newborn suck
and swallow
and sucking again.

And the woman waits,
counting the hour
as she has before.
It whines itself
into a first few twitches,
then fitful tremblings,
convulsing next
but not fully spent
until the blood
that mothers of girl babies know.

The petal mouth,
pink as rosebay,
gives up the first trickle,
and then her nose.
And soon the only sound
is the woman's spade
making a place
small and cold as her morning yield.

Colleagues

I cannot remember the anger beginning,
nor who disliked the other first.
But I know your constancy, know
so much about you: the good teeth
the yellow eyes, the pause when I speak.

Once you said you cannot sleep when dogs bark at night.

We've staked territories, made
watchful peace, and I no longer claw
halfmoons in my palm when you're near.

I learned distance from a father who drank,
from the husband divorced, and the lover who left.
I'll not be caged by anger.

Yet when dogs bark at night, I turn; I turn until I wake.

The Salutation

Deciding they should visit teach, Beth
dials Brother Evans to get the number
of someone in the Relief Society.
The listening Willene thinks
of her first attempts at Mormon salutation.
"Sister" was not so bad; everyone's met
a nun or heard someone's "Sister says."
But "Brother" meant revival tents,
collection plates, people of anchored
intelligence and soaring intent.

At church she'd said "Bishop" or "Elder"
or managed without salutation. But one day
at work, Willene needed to call Brother Bailey
because her throat was sore, and she wanted
to know if Four-in-One was OKAY even though
the label read CAFFEINE.

Brother Bailey counseled the young bishop
and everyone else. He and his wife
cleaned the chapel, and nobody littered it.
He'd joined the Church in England,
had been on three missions, and believed
man would not set foot on the moon
because God prescribed bounds. And so
did Brother Bailey. Willene knew that even
the Trinity would address him as BROTHER BAILEY.

She dialed, hoping he'd answer, but his wife
gave a prim, "Bailey's." Sister Bailey
probably did not know his first name. Willene
whispered, "Is Bro—" and her boss looked up.
Another try: "Is Brother?" Once again—this time
aspirating every dry syllable, "Is Brother Bailey
there?" Her boss grinned. Brother Bailey
was in. Four-in-One was out.

It took years before none of that mattered.
And how could small things have mattered so?
But they did. And maybe still do.
Or Willene would not smile at declining to tell
Beth just what's in the Grand Marnier truffle
Elise is dividing in three exact pieces.
The chocolate warming her tongue persuades
Willene that alcohol does not evaporate
when cooked. And keeping her small secret,
she links arms with the other two as they go off
to take the month's message to the shut-in
sisters, bedridden north of the Bowery.

Walking Provo Canyon

At dawn the wind
delivered the oaks
of their last papery leaves,

and I saw that someone had scattered
the hornet's nest you nailed
to the maple tree.

At the spot
where we saw the snake slip
its thin skin,
I stopped, listened

to the corn husks
we'd shucked east of the cabin.
They rattled the death of all green things.

At Utah Lake

Her nipples ripen in the October night
as the woman lifts her dress.

All fall she's waited this wash
of moonlight, the calm of a husband
with a farm paid off, the confidence
of the youngest son, married now.

The woman's eyes are luminous
as the last plums she canned
so ripe the pits split the skin.

It is all as she knew it would be,
a ruffle of foam at her toes, the only
other motion a blue throb in one wrist.

A slit opens in the dark skin
of the lake, and she slips in,
her mouth round and pale
                    as the waiting moon.

MARILYN MCMEEN BROWN

Grandmother

Were you cold?
I was cold and the wind was bitter
The canyon wide and deep and chill,
The cabin walls as thin as paper.
Hold my hand.
Yes, I will.

Were you sad?
Bent, like a flower
Blown in the salt marsh by a gale,
Bathed by the moon and the ice of a shower.
Warm my hand.
Yes, I will.

Were you ill?
Yes, ill and lonely,
Lying on the blackened floor,
The children crying, "Mother, mother!
Give us water. Give us more!"

Did you help them?
Yes, I gave them
The dregs of water from the well.
On my knees I crawled to bathe them,
Touch their lips with the empty pail.

Were you thirsty?
Yes, I thirsted,
But not for water, milk, or food;
I thirsted for my God's pure mercy.
Did he save you?
As he could.

Are you cold?
Yes, cold and lonely,
Walking toward the blowing night.
Have your warm hands come to take me?
Yes, that is right.

Will you Remember?

Will you remember, lovely love?
Before your kingdom come?
If you remember not one day
I remember one.

The sun and stars together
Beneath the deafening sky
Poured night and day and weather
Into a lovely cry.

And wild asparagus, rhubarb
Became our only meal.
We sat beneath the wattles
You built upon the hill.

You touched my hand and loved me.
I answered with a kiss.
You said, "I'm yours forever."
Do you remember this?

The rhubarb long has rotted,
The wattles tumbled through.
And so our love has died its death
And found its graveyard too.

We buried it in summer
Beneath the maple tree
About our shade and underneath
A short eternity.

Indian Playmate

When I go (be quiet, they told me)
To the river's edge by the Joshua wood
I often see you at daybreak
Climb from your sky-cold bed.

Holding tight to the black mane
Under my own black hair
Straight as thread
I come, quiet. Before the sunred
Wickiups, I spend
The morning, silent on my mare
Watching your ragged grandmothers stir
Water, and grind corn on stone—
On the morning air like ashes,
Shadows in the colored sun.

Hiding in the distant edge
Among the Joshua trees I feel
The sheep bones' beat
On the drum while I watch
You, sleep-eyed, come.

Your eyes, like mine, are black,
Your skin dust-worn.
You cling to your mother's colored skirts
Crusted with old mud
And tap with a sage-brush broom
Like ours at your yellow dog
That crowds the same frayed hens.
You dance and stamp and stir their wings.

You laugh like I laugh—
Your eyes slit, shine.
Your head, curl-shorn,
Bobs like the tail of a lamb
And you push the corn
Into your mouth with your thumb.

On the lean river
I see you squat in the brush.
You make the same boats I make
Out of leaves
And laugh them down the roiling length
I have not yet come.
Then, raising your eyes,
You catch my horse,
Sense in the distance—a mirror.
Not daring to sound
You spin away from the river
Toward the sand.

You, busy, build the same crumbling walls
I build out of the same slivers of stone.

VERNICE WINEERA PERE

Heritage

Take the sharpened pipi shell,
piece of paua, bird-bone,
razor-blade if you like.
Carve upon my face the marks
of Maoritanga. Let the blood spurt
and dribble down my chin
like the moko of the old women
wrapped in blankets round the cooking-fire.
Rub the juices in the wounds,
charcoal, vegetable dye, India ink.
Make beautiful the design, like
the young fern curled across the moon,
or the kiwi feathers in grandfather's proud cloak.
Seek the patterns of the paua's inner shell,
the curl of kumara vine.
Trace the call of the karanga across the marae,
the nose-flute in the night.
Slice the flesh like the teko-teko's stare.
The soft flesh, lip, membrane, skin.
Cut statistics on my face:
name, age, place of birth, race,
village, tribe, canoe.
Carve deeply, erase doubt
as to who
I am.
Use the sharpened pipi shell,
bird-bone, razor-blade.
Use them harshly, lacerate
my legacy upon me
where all who can read
will perceive that I am
taking my place on this vast marae
that is the Pacific.

At the Wall

It is 3:00 a.m. Shabbat.
Our last hour in Jerusalem.
O Jerusalem!
We crawl from the labyrinth
of cobblestones and arches
while cats and rubbish
lurk in narrow alleys.
We slink past soldiers
sleepless and sullen
in their makeshift box
drawn by vagrant dreams
to The Wall.

Under yellow lights it leans,
the old blocks huge
and bruised like human need.
The empty square rings beneath our feet.
No longer night, nor yet day,
limbo between heaven and earth
claims us. The Wall! The Wall!
A wail of longing in my soul
batters itself against these outsized bricks
and I would wrench prayers from my pride
and press them in paper-stuffed cracks
between my God and me.

Men are here, black clothed
and hatted, and small boys, heads
shaved, ringletted. Women too,
shawled and quiet.
Chastened, I wait
and watch till dawn responds
to murmured hope, the muttering of song,
the heart's chant in the hushed hour.
O, God of Jerusalem, Lord of all
this earth, hear my plea:
Let the wall between Thee and me
melt in mercy, and my praise
raze the rock of thine austerity!

Homecoming

(for my father)

I saw you as the tug
yet strained the ties
pulling her snug against the
timbered breast of that wild wharf.
From the city I arrived
with smoked cod and grapes
in the package between us,
amazed at the years age
had ground in your face.
We embraced,
a gull cried, the cold wind
cut from the sea.
Later, on the terrace,
salt-caked and crumbling
at the cliff's torn edge,
we ate, sheltered in the lee
of the wind's bruised kiss.
Peeling flesh from bones,
you pointed to old photos,
the leavings of your life.
I fingered the years between us
trying to appear wise
but all the while seeing you laid bare
like the fish now stripped of flesh
and your bleak stare
across an ocean, empty,
save for wind-whipped waves.

On Utah Lake

You laugh at my fear
of walking on water however
thick its winter skin,
while I marvel at your ability
to skirt the real issue
of fluid below, its echo
sounding, like whales in the deep
or some lost submarine testing the depth
of my faith.

On my feet the edges of knives, I repeat
the doubt I can even stand
above bubbles of air, fish, rocks,
weeds, and whatever else lies down there,
— let alone slide, walk, glide,
skate my way into grace!

Such slippery conceit. To think
one can imitate the feat
of God or angel or even, in this case,
friend. You are elegance itself,
at one with the elements of air and sky
and I, my heart filled with love,
can only watch you glide by, smiling,
willing me out onto ice.

Dignity eludes me. At the deep
green of the middle of lake
I come to a halt, and like
the fabled centipede unable to figure
which foot to put first, I freeze
against a lowering sky
and hear the honking of geese
who rise like a cloud in the cold
and call to me, "Come, fly!"

Half-caste

Here, beside the creek,
where past events float by
like fallen leaves
soggy now
with the weight of water
heavier, certainly, than tears.
Here is where Kahui hit me
with my own school bag,
the blow didn't hurt
it was something else
that stung my eyes.
Closer to the source
watercress grows
green with the taste of spring
and Maoritanga.
Up in the bush we washed our feet
and hands stained with blackberry juice
then walked out, billy cans full,
following the creek to find the pa again.
We choose our own crosses to bear
heavy as the square timbers
that form this bridge
across the chuckling water
as we grow.
Mine was to know
how it feels to have one leg
on one side of a river,
one on the other
and never quite belong
on either side.
How wide the water
between the child
and growing up;
pride and shame;
my Maori name and white face;
neither race completely claiming
a half-caste child
so lacking grace.

Blue Her Eyes

In a world of brown
her eyes were blue upon the mending
of pants, the darning of socks,
the turning of collars until
no fabric remained.
Blue like the wool she knitted
by the fire those afternoons
when summer had fled
the windswept coast
and I came home from school
to cocoa and the chores of gathering wood
and carrying coal.
Blue like the heavy grey-blue eggs
the ducks hid in their hedge-row nests
I hunted, filling the old kit carefully,
knowing beforehand the thick yolk-
covered bread and salted homemade butter
taste of breakfast.
Blue, her eyes,
like the paua's look
upon the coffin of her son
mourned on the marae
and laid beside his father
in this colonial earth so far away
from that bright nation of her birth.
Blue, her eyes,
blue as the brittle teacup locked
in the windowed cabinet
with the tiny key, safe
from a grandchild's searching
for tokens of identity.

Blue, her eyes.

SALLY T. TAYLOR

Embryo

Creation.
Before it is, it moves.
Does it think as it
    turns its face?
Is its knee-jerk reflex?

What happens at these
    fibrillations?
Do teaspoon hands cup,
and fingers feel each
    its own movement?

It is still just before
the exodus, when the water
turns to blood.

        Firstborn,
the angel of death
stands ready before dawn.

Labor

Mountains cup the patchwork
sewn by ancestors. Skyline
road edges the east, and straight-
seamed roads bisect the acres.

They feel the comfort of familiar
trees and banks of useful streams.
Through the glass, they watch
neighbors' lights disappear. Together

in the center of the valley, center
of the house, center of the bed,
they touch in darkness, feeling
knobs of knots on the tied quilt.

She watches the movement of the clock
and curls silently with the waves.
There is yet time. He rises on an elbow,
then turns to cushion her back.

Fading Family Portrait

Lifting her paper bones so she can lie
On thick pillows, you bring your mother's tray,
Thinking of the unanswered question — why?

She eats a bite or two, then turns to cry.
You draw the drapes against the failing day.
Lifting her paper bones so she can lie

Again supine, you set the dinner by
And smooth her hair. You ponder death's delay,
Thinking of the unanswered question. Why

Does she live, lingering when she wants to die?
You touch away her tears. What can you say?
Lifting her paper bones so she can lie

Straight and flat, you sit a moment more, sigh,
And let the ragged thoughts come as they may,
Thinking of the unanswered question. Why

Is it said that suffering can sanctify
The soul? You feel her consummate dismay,
Lifting her paper bones so she can lie
Thinking of the unanswered question — why?

Before I Was Born, My Father

In a darkened room, I saw

my father for the first time:
    a movie clip
come by accident into my hands,
    a movie clip
not more than two minutes long

    taken before his death
    when I was two
taken even before my birth,

my older sisters
        clinging to his legs
        a younger one in his arms.

He smiled
        in the film.

    Taller and more handsome
than I had
        guessed — he
was the father I only faintly remember
        perhaps.

My father
    smiling before I
            was born

A shade
    moving in black and white

the face that I had dreamed.

PENNY ALLEN

The Word was Unperfected Till Made Flesh

The word was unperfected till made flesh:
With clay and spittle Christ restored the blind;
He laid his hands on those whom he would bless;
His body bled as he redeemed mankind.

As "Hamlet" issued forth from words and time
Or "David" was released from faulty stone,
So soul and body can become sublime;
The Spirit follows passion's path in bone.

Desired, fathered, and resired, then born
In blood that craves both earth and sky, we'd love
With heart, might, mind and strength; yet torn,
Abuse the means by which we'd rise above,

Refuse and swill and rut: damn the divine,
As devils still desire to enter swine.

Blackberry

Sucking darkness into swollen lobes,
It rides the cane over in its plumpness.
She wants it — enough to thread a careful hand
Through the thorns, etching a ragged red
Rivulet on the wrist and pricking tiny
Rubies where she wavers until her fingers
Lightly pluck it — thumb-pad pierced by a point
In the process. She pulls the berry back
Through close-woven briars; it stains startled
Fingers pinching at the pull of a thorny

Anchor. She plunks it into her wet mouth.
Delicious. More desirable than the first
Death she ate. Yet long after her tongue
Forgets the sweet, her throbbing thumb remembers
The pain, and still hungry, into the tangle
She flinches, sighing, "Oh, Eden, Eden."

Tefnut

Tefnut, the Great Mother, came weeping to Egypt
    In those before times, but soon laughed,
    For through her sons a new line began,
Not the fathers' line, but Pharaohs called her
    Mother, sacrificing children, seeking
    The secret of the patriarchal key word.

Hathor, Ishtar, Freya, Durga, and Kali,
    She was Anath, consort and mother of Baal,
    Ashtoreth over Moloch. She was Eve.
What secrets did she insist on knowing
    When she took the fruit? Made to be a
    Helpmeet, she helped Adam out of Eden.

Mother of all but that parentless power he forfeits
    When dominion and compulsion weigh
    The soul, how can she make him just—as she
Would be? Wrestle an angel? What did Hagar
    Want from Abraham for Ishmael that the
    Father saved for ancient Sarah's son?

Is it the power to throw upon a wheel
    A world? To set the time for stars to burst
    As signs to man? To spin the earth in space,
To make the sun stand still and mountains move,
    Practicing not on mountains but on clods?
    What is such power to one who makes the mover?

I Will One Day Be a Widow, Love

I will one day be a widow, love;
Statistics cast that solitary role.
A wind will catch your reaching boughs and shove,
Ripping entwined roots from our shared soil.
From sharpest winds I shelter in your lee
And drink the rain that slides from your cupped leaves,
Yet your trunk's strength is doubled beside me;
Your pollen turns eternal in my seeds.
Not like the twining ivy, borrowing height,
That heaps upon the ground with the tree's fall,
When your support is gone, I'll still use light
And sway with circling seedlings and grow tall.
I'll branch the gap and find the seasons sweet,
But miss you, miss you, never quite complete.

Drought

Drought has withered the city's strident stalks.
Vining cables sag, then fall in tangled heaps
Among chitinous husks of cars and trucks.
Flurries of window panes above the streets
Scintillate in sunlight as they fall;
They gently shatter on decayed cement,
Merging into mulch with stone and steel.
Rusting girders wilt in passive want.
For we had paved our glittering lakes of corn,
Stopped our fruitful springs, and damned our wheat,
Soiled the sea and let the breakers burn
When fertilizer seemed our greatest need.
But malls were grown from aquifers of grain;
From rivers of plankton, teeming towers sprang.

Post Partum Blues

Uncomfortable companions in the
Pulse of days
Since first I felt you kicking
At my walls,
Pushing from my surface to
Define your own,
Your growing stretched me
Beyond my bound,
Rooted you to me in
Transient need.
Bearing down against myself
To see you freed,
I thought the pain of parting
Worth the bearing,
But when, now you've gone, will I
Stop tearing?

The Coyote

Enemy of sheep,
Who would believe
You lair in canyons
Overlooked by houses
Whose wide windows yearn
For meadows of lights?
You slink among tams and marigolds
Glutting on garbage and stray kittens,
Seducer of pedigreed bitches.

R. A. CHRISTMAS

Ghost truck
for RHC

Now I lay me down by the freeway,
in a duplex in Cedar City, Utah;

and twenty yards west of these bricks
rides the asphalt, as high as my roof,

where the line-haul drivers trade leads
all night in their big sets of doubles.

I slide back the window and listen
for morning on my grandfather's freight dock:

hand-trucks thumping past my head;
unloading those box-cars of Sno-jel;

Grandpa pissed off at everybody;
my father hunched over the bill-writer;

Racer, and Herb, and Conley;
the hay-truck that burned on the Grapevine —

we were watching the hot tires explode
when a semi came honking down the grade

with brakes lit like torches, dodging
the blazing bales on the road.

Sometimes, when it's snowing, I wake
in the darkness of morning and listen

so far into the fall of a snowflake
that the plows have given up for the night,

and the lanes are as quiet as trails
under snow that will never go home.

I put down my ear to the white line
and listen all the way to California,

for the ghost-truck driven by my father
through the orange groves, Route 66,

on the two-lane from Barstow to Vegas,
then he compounds up the Black Ridge,

climbing the white grade into Cedar —
was there something he promised to bring me?

The dash-lights flicker in the cab;
I can see, through the sleep in his eyes,

the young hands, a green pack of Luckies,
these towns that he doesn't understand:

Kanarraville, Hamilton Fort —
he thinks of polygamy, and chuckles.

The old International looms closer;
it stops on the shoulder above me.

In the pale yellow glow of the trailer,
he gets out, whacks the tires all around,

vaults the guard-rail, comes down to the fence,
and listens for the sound of my breathing.

His fingers hooked into the chain-links;
in the cold his sighs are like plumes —

dry flakes dusting his hair;
I lie here, waiting and listening.

"Remember the war?" he begins.
"I'm sorry I wasn't a soldier."

"I remember it some," I answer.
"I carried a candle in the blackout,

when the Japs didn't bomb L.A."
"I had a bad ear," he continues,

"and my left eye wouldn't sit straight.
So mostly I remember driving,

coffeeshops, unloading in Frisco —
I drove Tojo into the ground."

"I waited for you," I reply,
"the shape of your headlights in the darkness,

after Cub Scouts, after the games,
after church, after everything.

I waited for you like a demon."
"Don't wait," he whispers, "anymore."

"I remember one morning," I say.
"Mom standing at a sun-struck window,

Crying, with the phone in her hand.
'The war is over,' she said."

At Mountain Meadows

for Juanita Brooks

The mass grave here is set with stones
piled low inside a low rock wall,
and marked for travelers by a sign
that tells us briefly of the murder
of six score emigrants, whose bones
once lay all over — on the plain
and in the gulley — left to the weather
of almost a century where they fell

like so many others, screaming, shot,
robbed and left naked in the dust;
a few of the millions underneath,
and killed for something, like the rest
that we remember and forget
in stone and plaque — our modern shrines,
a casual pilgrimage of death
for tourists in the summertime

who cannot stay to sift for those
ungathered pieces of the dead
that wash out here in summer floods
like parts of broken animals,
but choose a few things to take home,
the date, a name, then pass adept
as visitors around low walls,
inspecting what they must disown;

forgetting that such ways will end
when these bones, bursting to rebirth,
pick through the meadows for debris
we did not number, and the Earth
burns to a glass in which we see
ourselves as we are seen, wherein
we read, as guilt and innocence,
the record of our ignorance.

Self-portrait as Brigham Young

He pioneered his name into the Church.
His family said, "You're nuts!" —
so he set off alone. He was eighteen.

On the first day out, he got lost;
and for the next twenty-seven years
he wandered the wicked West, left

two wives and two children on the trail,
and almost forgot his calling —
till he stumbled, at last, on the Valley.

Ill and exhausted, in a station-wagon
with five kids who wouldn't settle,
he gazed at the Great City.

The Temple had been finished long ago,
and some of the old streets
looked as tired as he felt

after sixteen hours on the Interstate
without a cigarette —
but he was proud of that.

"This is still the right place,"
he announced to his squirming children.
"Drive on. Drive on."

In Beaver Canyon

for William Stafford

Driving down Beaver Canyon, Bill,
I caught two deer in my lights: a doe
and her fawn. I stopped to let them cross
over to the stream to get their drink.

But you know how it is—they spooked
at the edge of the pavement, at a loss
for aspen, and began a slow
confused meandering, until

they found the other side, and stood still
in my blinding bath of light. And so
I drove them—they could not pass
into their darkness down the bank.

Just where that safety began, they shrank
and skittered like a couple of calves.
Finally I figured what to do,
and turned my lights off—like a fool

if someone came barreling down the hill;
and suddenly I could sense no more
than the night air, and the grinding wash
where the canyon blackness hid the creek.

I waited patiently in that dark
for about ten seconds, then felt for the dash
and set my brights again—the doe
was dropping away; I saw her tail,

the trees, the white line—but the fawn fell
on the shoulder, scrambled, turned to go
the wrong way, jumping, hit by the flash.
Then he came on a dead-run for the truck.

Forgive me, Bill,
but this was a time to save a buck.
I turned them off again—and the cuss
swerved—in mid-air—and just grazed my door,
leaving me thankful, dark and still.

To the Sound of the Rain

I want to love you tonight
To the sound of the rain.

I want to be
Roof and walls to you,
And burning wood.

I want you to see my smile
For a second of lightning.

I want you to hear
The steady beat of my heart
Between the thunder
And my voice
Whispering your name
And almost silent kisses
As I love you tonight
To the sound of the rain.

Guilt

I have no vulture sins, God,
That overhang my sky,
To climb, grey-feathering the air,
And swoop carnivorously.

It's just the tiny sins, God,
That from memory appear
Like tedious, buzzing flies to dart
Like static through my prayer.

Millie's Mother's Red Dress

It hung there in the closet
While she was dying, Mother's red dress,
Like a gash in the row
Of dark, old clothes
She had worn away her life in.

They had called me home,
And I knew when I saw her
She wasn't going to last.

When I saw the dress, I said,
"Why, Mother—how beautiful!
I've never seen it on you."

"I've never worn it," she slowly said.
"Sit down, Millie—I'd like to undo
A lesson or two before I go, if I can."

I sat by her bed,
And she sighed a bigger breath
Than I thought she could hold.
"Now that I'll soon be gone,
I can see some things.
Oh, I taught you good—but I taught you wrong."

"What do you mean, Mother?"

"Well—I always thought
That a good woman never takes her turn,
That she's just for doing for somebody else.
Do here, do there, always keep
Everybody else's wants tended and make sure
Yours are at the bottom of the heap.
Maybe someday you'll get to them,
But of course you never do.
My life was like that—doing for your dad,
Doing for the boys, for your sisters, for you."

"You did—everything a mother could."

"Oh, Millie, Millie, it was no good—
For you—for him. Don't you see?
I did you the worst of wrongs.
I asked nothing—for me!

"Your father in the other room,
All stirred up and staring at the walls—
When the doctor told him, he took
It bad—came to my bed and all but shook
The life right out of me. 'You can't die,
Do you hear? What'll become of me?
What'll become of me?'
It'll be hard, all right, when I go.
He can't even find the frying pan, you know.

"And you children.
I was a free ride for everybody, everywhere.
I was the first one up and the last one down
Seven days out of the week.
I always took the toast that got burned,
And the very smallest piece of pie.
I look at how some of your brothers treat their wives now,
And it makes me sick, 'cause it was me
That taught it to them. And they learned.
They learned that a woman doesn't
Even exist except to give.
Why, every single penny that I could save
Went for your clothes, or your books,
Even when it wasn't necessary.
Can't even remember once when I took
Myself downtown to buy something beautiful—
For me.

"Except last year when I got that red dress.
I found I had twenty dollars
That wasn't especially spoke for.
I was on my way to pay it extra on the washer.
But somehow — I came home with this big box.
Your father really gave it to me then.
'Where you going to wear a thing like that to —
Some opera or something?'
And he was right, I guess.
I've never, except in the store,
Put on that dress.

"Oh, Millie — I always thought if you take
Nothing for yourself in this world,
You'd have it all in the next somehow.
I don't believe that anymore.
I think the Lord wants us to have something —
Here — and now.

"And I'm telling you, Millie, if some miracle
Could get me off this bed, you could look
For a different mother, 'cause I would be one.
Oh, I passed up my turn so long
I would hardly know how to take it.
But I'd learn, Millie.
I would learn!"

It hung there in the closet
While she was dying, Mother's red dress,
Like a gash in the row
Of dark, old clothes
She had worn away her life in.

Her last words to me were these:
"Do me the honor, Millie,
Of not following in my footsteps.
Promise me that."

I promised.
She caught her breath,
Then Mother took her turn
In death.

MARGARET RAMPTON MUNK

For Russ

If they asked me
How I know
You will be true,
What would I say?

Because of what I am?
More beautiful
And more alluring wives
Have been betrayed.

Because of what you've promised?
A broken promise
Is as common
As a trampled blade of grass.

Because of what you fear?
You are not one to relish rumors
Of another's error,
Or fear the whispers
Of your own.

Because of what you are—
This is my assurance.
On your birthday,
Thank you for this gift to me,
This and every year.

from "One Year"

I. *The Beginning*

Such things ought not to happen
In the spring.

The white azaleas bloomed
In honor of my going,
And I left them knowing
They and I would be alike depleted
At my coming home.

Tomorrow marks a stepping down
From prayer to resignation;
The final period
To hope.

II. *The News*

The scene was written
In advance,
Rehearsed as often
As the days of waiting
Would allow.

The curtains of sedation
Would be parted to reveal
My husband's face,
The good news broadcast
From his eyes,

Voice buoyant with the word,
Among the loveliest bequeathed
By Roman tongue to Saxon —
Benign:
>   Of a kind disposition;
>   Manifesting gentleness and mildness;
>   Tending to promote well-being;
>   Beneficial.

And I would bathe
The hard, brusque pillow
With some grateful tears,
Burrow into healing sleep,
And wake to life resumed.

Instead,
Along the timeless, lightless hours
Spanning days and nights indifferently,
The sluggish curtain lifted,
Hesitated,
Fell,
And lurched again,
Three times allowing glimpses
Of a vision so unwelcome
That narcosis masqueraded ably
As a fair seducer,
Come to lure me back.

The face was right,
The eyes were there,
The voice.
The word was wrong.
Malignant:
    Showing great malevolence;
    Actively evil in nature;
    Threatening to life or health;
    Deadly.

The third time,
The drug had lost its power
To be kind.
I knew.
Each morning I would wake
And know again,
And mornings would become a year
In which this once familiar body,
Turned traitor
Only halfway through the course,
Would be a battleground.

The cue was wrong for tears.
They waited, prisoners behind
A hard tube filling up
The passageway of sound.
So pain became
The gaoler of grief,
And I lay silently,
Rewriting.

IV. *The Nurses*

I will forget their names,
But not the kind brown hands
Applying dignity
Along with soap and lotion;
The quiet voices of experience,
Soothing shock and terror
With the balm perspective;
The shoulder into which at last,
The night I saw the truth
Inscribed on paper
In the correspondence
Of consoling friends,
I unleashed ten days' hoard
Of tears.

Never mattered less
The color of the hands,
The accent of the voice.
Never had I learned
From solemn ceremony,
Quilting bees,
Or angry feminist crusades
What helplessness and pain
Taught me of sisterhood.

V. *The Hair*

I always had some,
Even in my youngest picture.

After it had darkened,
My parents told me how
They once could hide a penny
Of new copper there
Among the strands.

It grew prolifically haphazard
Down a shy and conscientious
Schoolchild's back,
And hung below my waist
In auburn ropes
Plaited during every breakfast
By my mother's fingers.
Once,
I purposely released the bands
And let the waves fall free
Until the teacher
Bound them back.

At Easter,
Armed with cotton rags,
Like a determined healer
Binding up some annual wound,
My mother operated on a kitchen stool
Until it hung in shampooed corkscrews,
Ribboned to accentuate
The spring's new dress.

At eleven,
Sharp pain on the right became
Three days of tossing
In a hard hospital bed,
While woven braids dissolved into
A tangled nest I knew to be
Beyond redemption.
A kind nurse found me crying.
Did it hurt so much?
When I confessed
The honest cause of tears,
She sat an hour beside me
With a brush,
And not the scissors I had feared.

That summer
As a sacrifice
To junior high,
I underwent a second surgery,
And had them severed
At the shoulders,
To appear three decades later
In a Christmas box
Sent by my mother
To my daughter.

When we met,
My husband called it red.
I grew it long again
For him.

Today I combed it,
Clipped and brittle and drug-dead,
Into a basket
In the bathroom
Of my mother's home.
And she who placed the penny,
Wrapped the rags,
Preserved the plaits,
Joined me in mourning.

VI. *The Interloper*

When my husband went to bed in summer,
It was with another woman.

I hardly envied her.
She was less
Than I had been in spring.
Lighter by ten pounds,
Thin and scarred and hollowed out,
Both outward crown
And inward parts
That marked her as a woman
Gone.

This time the doctor
Was a lawyer,
His only remedy
The loving instinct
Of a man two decades married.

His sudden ardor
For his strange new partner
Was transparent, but
Remarkably effective.

X. *New England Country Graveyard on an Autumn Day*

How much is spoken
By grey stone
Where time and rain
Have left it still articulate.

Too often,
As I stroll and read
By mellow light
Of mid-October,
The message is
The brevity of life.

This one was someone's wife,
But only long enough
To bear her man one child,
And bring it that same day
To sleep beside her here.

This one,
Despite the promise
And the strivings of a boy,
Lived long enough to be a soldier—
Never quite a man.

This couple lie
With tiny, grass-bound slabs
Strung like a rosary
At the parental feet.
How much life was left
In hearts too often pierced
Before they followed to this place
The children
Whom they should have left behind?

God, God!
Not yet!
Keep me longer
From the darkness of those beds.
And when the colors on these hills
Are gone, and green,
And gold again,
Let me be here to see
With open eyes
And well-loved people
Just a call away.

XI. *Remission*

These luminous November days,
A bonus bought with suffering and prayer,
Linger on as if they were aware
Of winter grief their dear tenacity delays.

Recalled to scenes I feared forever gone,
I cry to every shining leaf, "Hold on! Hold on!"

DIXIE LEE PARTRIDGE

Wilderness

A Sacramento family camps on vacation
in Oregon. Their five-year-old vanishes
one smoky evening while they cook trout.
They stay on at the same campsite
as searchers cover the September countryside for miles.
Weeks pass. The flawless trees go on
with their silent enterprise above and beneath
the forest floor, keeping what the people seek
but fear to know. Birds and small animals
communicate their cries through darkening
days. It's nearly winter.
The people do not want to go home.

I remember a late night long ago,
being brought home from a movie I'd slept through.
Our door had blown open during a light blizzard —
the farmhouse stood dark and gaping,
a shallow drift across its floor.
I huddled on a straight-back chair, arms
around my knees, not wanting my feet to touch
the strange snow. I watched my mother
sweep it through the doorway, wipe linoleum
and chair legs before she helped me
into cold pajamas and sheets that had frozen
on her line before being brought inside to dry.
I wanted never to think about that cold again.

Winter Horses

for my father, who farmed
with horses into the 70s.

West of home, Horse Heaven Hills
slope into wide, low sky.
They winter gracefully: coats
whitened, their range subtle
with desert brush and the flat,
iron lay of boreal rivers.

Far up the eastward tributary,
my father's draft teams also winter.
In light made blue
from snow and distant pine,
they wait the night along fences,
coats thickened under hoarfrost, breath
ghosting toward the north:
the ancient, slow stamp of feet heavy
with the woolly mammoth's.

They live always in the distance,
the cold around them warmer
for their faint steam, their rest
ongoing, upright, a part of all
winter landscapes. I know they lie down
to give birth or to die.

Snowy Owl
At Woodland Park Zoo

Stoic, he eyes
the curious and the unimpressed alike —
a white prince,
origins of captivity scattered
like rubbish on pavements
circling, circling. . . .
Within smeared glass,
bearded claws commemorate
the casual nests, private young.

I tell myself I've humanized the owl,
born to this habitat
like I to twentieth-century man,
bloodlines stretched thin,
beyond origins of conscience —
what we are meant to be
winging, distant on the pale horizon;
what we are becoming
soundlessly approaching
unseen, to fall
accurate on its prey.

Quickening

My ribs remember . . . you thumped
against night. First-year cries invade it.
You attack day before first light, dishevel crib,
ransack the house at your level: raccoon ritual.
In the yard you finger fence-links,
learning edges.

Your walk is run and stumble;
carried, you push legs against me, pump
us like a hand car down some endless track.
Even your hugs are kinetic, hands
patting my shoulder blades,
knees pushing up, fetal.

Poking buttons until we play
your music — switched-on Bach or Mills piano —
you sit center-floor to wave the beat.
When brown eyes glaze with fought-off sleep
you let me cradle you, arms
flailing.

At last you quiet. I hold
the moment: body easing to mine, breath matching.
I deliver you to bed, smell dampness
at your hairline; you quiver
a slight moan, like a small animal,
dying.

Learning to Quilt

Time goes one way only, but we
go two: . . . we drowse in care of our dreams—
their sheltering flamboyant wings
stretched over us, one in the past
and one in the future.
                    —WILLIAM MATTHEWS

The patchwork, stretched on frames,
crowds furniture and all essential work
to edges; farmhouse windows in old lace
cast filigree on pastels of *nine-patch-stars.*
"You need a thimble," says my mother,
pleased to pass on the tiny stitches
that hold a quilt for generations.

Pattern names are italic in my memory:
the rambler, jacob's ladder, flock-of-geese,
but I can't place them with their quilts—
my grandmothers gone, Aunt Lena 82,
Mary in her final bed with cancer.
I imagine them wrapped in quilts
in their graves, carrying the permanence
of fingers ever stitching,
ever certain.

Nights, we are hemmed to dreams
overlaid with the calico and flannel
of distant relatives; appliques
from christening gowns, the old wools
of the fathers' first suits.

A Woman Dreams of Her Daughter, Born with Down's Syndrome

At the far end of twin lakes, you spend
summer weekends, sleeping in a tent,
though she would rather be out with the stars
and doesn't mind rain. In your dream you see her
coming toward you from the boat dock,
her walk even and straight: no side to side

movement of the body, her voice and form
without thickness. You have dreamed her
this way for years, familiar
and agile as the squirrels that eat
from her hand, chestnut-eyed
with deer that shy from your table.

Her hand is cupped with its offering
of petals: yellow from the wildness
of rose thickets below the ridge. She places
a single petal on her tongue, on your eyelids
like a benediction, her hair bowed
to where you lie in the sun

and you jolt awake.
She is standing by the cot watching
your sleep, her grin widening
with the morning, her silence allowing you
the utterance of lake waters, ovations
from the pools of pre-dawn light.

STEPHEN GOULD

Tribunal Alien

The City of Peace.
Linger, still, in sections of the light
trees and the shadows of trees,
the ancient tunnel and the pool beyond the wall,
Siloam. Still in the unstirred morning, girls
carry water from the pool; still, at Jerusalem
City Hall, the Chamber of Commerce is met
for the day of the Lord's condemnation.

But this city westward, not of peace,
weaves its walls into the stuff of life:
wealth and squalor, private faces, daily news.
The hush of news is speechlessness afoot,
that girls may avoid the streets at night;
the wind drives wandering men along the streets
and men and women in the streets are wry reflections
like minor bleeding about the fingernails.

Suspicion sustains a man in his crime.
If he lifts his face when you pass him in the streets
you may see a webwork of lines
crossed as the roads by which he passes you,
intersected as the ways he followed until
one betrayed him, he tore himself open,
and the blood flows continually out of him:
you may see he suspects you, Mirror of Sores,
Pool to Whom he Cannot Flow.

He sleeps in parks, or by sun-heated walls,
in the daytime; moves south in the winter.
He remembers himself in wildernesses
finally obdurate. I remember him in judgments
of the night, and disinclined, I think instead
of my own possible soul: I say,
In your release are the forbiddings in my flesh,
Barabbas, brother.

Sabbath Flower

I.

It is all grown quiet;
even
the last soft spadefallen soil
is settled, is quiet.

The congregated celebrants
in passing
from their own seed-time
germinate beneath their taken wind.

Let omen be the name of spirit:
the seed-place passes
in its time.

This is a street-corner funeral.
Behind the heavy plate-glass windows
lettered gold on black
mimicries, false shadows of letters,
the funerary audience masses,
drugged for sacrifice, withheld
among our bitter or our sweetened drinks
from gusts that flex the glass, quake
rampant at its barrier.
The victim
has named me master
of sacrifices, the priest. I am to know,
but bite the silence in my mouth.

II.

That bridge that is the work of hands
admits the stream beneath;
this bridge that is the work of hands
purports the traffic of our feet—
beneath the bridge, our flower-boats
and from the bridge false lovers watch
our sport of men.

This is a winter-bound island
and awning. People
here in meadows, hills, populations, streets, doorways, solitudes
braid cables of their dawn and dusk of voices
coil the cables on the sidewalk
under the dripping awning.
There are no strangers in the neighborhood today —
there is no one to be recognized as strange.
A German shepherd on a leash has nuzzled
at the hands within his tether's range,
received no food;
sits by his mistress's leg.

III.

That bridge that is the work of time
is mark and pace-mark of the flow:

across the wooden arch across the stream
we gathered the flowers and we wove the garland
for the neck and shoulders of bronze
steadfast Buddha:
the shrine today is redwood benches, jasmine
tea and fortune cookies

and we watch the naked sparrows, just
beyond us, wet, and picking seeds.

The batter of iron on iron sides,
the clatter of anchor-chains
is the censer, diesel-smoke the incense,
garland and life-ring,
rescue of broken packing crates
and styrofoam cups near an oil slick.

IV.

Let flower be the name of seed-time,
seed the time.
The omen is the bird's blood-flashing wing.
The garden is the Buddha,
bronze the garden's child:

three
whirl-winds flank
an ornamental pond
on a cold,
haze-buried day.
That central walks the water
and grows white; those
flanking follow, right and left; they
lock their triangle
with that of glancing shadows in the pond.
Let omen be the name of spirit.
Then

all is grown quiet, even
as the named immersion's prayer
is growing, still.

Fish Census

Cicadas in the dry pines overhead; vortex
dimples like trouts' pocks mark the last
water at the pumphead till the pump sucks air;
he shuts it down; in the dry shadows a reflex,
silence to repose, washes in the locusts' lisp
like the final gurge of water from the lines over
the pumphead when the pump kicks back to the exhaust
stroke and the tree-shades touch wisps of drying algae.

We have trout in buckets of warm
water taken from the stream in the cool morning;
we pitch away the last water from the hole
with cans, to count the sculpins. Flies swarm
on our bare backs like a malaise of slight poisoning
present as wrecked marmots on stone slopes.

Group Session

An hour and a half,
the conversation wooden, constrained,
I did not find my others there.
I might have been

someone else's chiseled notes
struck, passing, to request its shape
of an unresolving stone;
at the end I walked away.

I walked downhill. Obliged,
I bought my food prepared, and then
scion of a family old as man
I eat this food in hunger,

but without the appetite for it.

COLIN B. DOUGLAS

Take, Eat

Like a deer he comes to me,
Parting the ferns,
Like a deer with bright antlers.
I chase him across meadows,
Beside streams I pursue him,
And he does not weary.
But in the thicket he surprises me;
He lets my arrow pierce him.
He gives me of his flesh at evening,
And in the bright morning,
Like a deer he comes to me.

Adoni: Cover Me with Thy Robe

Adoni: Cover me with thy robe;
Let me rest against thee.
I have traveled in far places;
Where thou hast sent me, I have gone.
Among serpents I have laid my bed;
I have risen to go among wolves.
I have walked in dry places
Where the rocks held no water;
I have climbed high mountains
Where frost was my covering.
I have gone unshod;
My feet have bled.
I am weary;
I have found no rest.
Let me rest against thee.
Shelter me with thy robe.

Wedding Songs

1

On the first morning of our marriage,
You gave me raspberries in a white bowl.
Later we stood barefoot on sand
And let white seafoam wash about our ankles.

2

We lay down among flowers,
The grass sweet and wet,
Your dress wet.
Horses came near under blue sky,
Treading down the sweet grass,
And your dress was yellow among the flowers.

3

The whiteness of foam,
The smell of morning rain;
And as we walked on the sand,
My fingertips touched your sleeve.

4

I come with gifts of milk and wine,
Silver shoes, and a bough of cherries,
And enter your garden of roses.

5

Your hand through the parted veil,
And later, the forked flame of your thighs.
Sarai's limbs in Abram's tent
Could not have burned more bright.

BRUCE W. JORGENSEN

On Second West in Cedar City, Utah: Canticle for the Virgin

Ave Maria, plena gratia!

One street west, in the ward chapel,
I reinforce with paper thimble
of water and shard of bread
my bond to God:
precarious grace, when
thewed will stranded on bones
must vault the horns
of His justice and mercy
to turn redemption's temporal trick.

I would not go this street to prayer,
yet passing in a cold morning
I make prayer here:
praise for plastic flowers
writhen beneath your feet
and fading in suppliant hands
under your alabastrine gaze,
for which also praise
and praise for this small lapse

in the disquietude of God.

Weight of Glory

Those I must leave
Are all that I would have
When I ascend
Alone into love.

Gathering Apples in First Snow

This year October takes us sudden, breaks
The honeylocust leaves with a parching frost
And casts them, ashen green and clattering, down
On sidewalks still glaring as white as summer.
My calendar, thumbtacked beside the scarred
Refrigerator door, spells out September.
I lift the leaf: improvidence this first
Year in a rented house with garden (plowed
When I came, but unsown) and five apple trees,
Their bearing laced (I sprayed too late) with worms.

The west of afternoon draws dark; I'm picking
The last apples, some rotten on the stem,
Others by birds half hollowed, good flesh ridged
And seared. Leave those. Still on the tree some stems
Do not give easy, and I let fall into
A rainwarped cardboard box twigs and the bitten
Leaves with sound fruit—too far not to bruise, from
This muddy rung. Silence. Around me, in
The tree, the snow starts falling, ticking like
Sand spilled on parchment, salt on old oilcloth.

Friends: a Moral Song

They had not meant,
Yet she in him as he in her
Saw what wishes might concur
If once they would relent

In eye or tongue
Or slack the rein keeping them yet
At stolid walk. But still they met
In halls, at doors, among

The selves they packed
To clothe their lovely selves, fearing
How skin sang and heart hearing
Pranced, cantered and bucked.

They did not kiss,
Though once, his finger near her mouth,
Knuckle to nail she let her breath
Kindle his bone. Nor this,

He thought, would crack
Him into speech, had not she then
Shivered and ducked her head again
And made to leave. Her back

To him, he called
Her back to him, her name that now
He spoke as if heart-stricken how
Quickly they two must fall

And so become
Lovers, if in mind alone,
Sharing the guilt without the sin,
Warding each other's blame.

A Litany for the Dark Solstice

Dead of winter,
Dead of night,
Neither center,
Left, nor right.

Teach me error
Within reason;
Stay me with terror
Out of season.
When I have most,
Whirl it as dust.
Salt be the taste
Of all I love best
In earth, and rust
Be the iron I trust.

In my distress,
Bless me to bless.
On urgent water,
Gone oar and rudder,
Still me this rest:

Break me to Christ.

DENNIS CLARK

For Anders at Seventy Days

Watching you nap open-mouthed on the couch reminds me,
warm in the noon-lit October room, of our walks,
nights when you're fretful, under the open sky,
to purge the smells of cooking, clatter of eating,
bloom of electric bulbs, so we can sleep.
        Something caught in your gut will give you no rest
although you've suckled your fill. It stretches and cramps
and twists you, trying to fit and tuck itself
in for the night. Lit by the sun it twitches
your lip and right arm, solemnly proving your nap;
shudders and sighs through your work of sorting the scenes
glowing behind the pink map of your unfolded lids
and the echoing shapes of our speech in the room of your brain.
        Whatever it is yields at night to the cold
and dark of our dry planet, the dance of our walk,
the tongue of my words—but most, I believe, to the stars.
Something about the unroofed house around us,
open space enough to house the soul,
lit with the distant ice of reticent stars,
calms you enough to launch you into sleep.
        Dolphin in the ocean of our dream,
you drift in our room all night, surfacing fitfully,
gasping after a breath of that open air.

Song for His Left Ear

for Harlow Soderborg Clark,
surgically deaf

By sheer nerve you've gone Van Gogh one better:
cut your ear off from your brain, but
left it blooming in your hair.
You'd auditioned city living nineteen years —
till thickened by the screech, slam, purr and snarl of traffic
one nerve sent early warning,
spun the city past your eyes,
milking your fear of falling and scalding the fall with fear.
The diagnosis came round with Thanksgiving.

Now there's twice the life to hear with one ear shot.
Your surgeon only cut the old line out
in his New Year's resolution of your lost tangle with balance;
his Christmas mining of the flesh against your skull
gave you full control of what you choose to hear . . .
as well as what you hear because it's there.

You can listen for the fog that muffles headlights,
hear the current surge on filament and singe,
throwing the world's shadow on the fabric of your mind;
you can hear Beethoven as he heard himself —
with the advantage of one ear for what musicians hear.
In the basement cool of your bed at night
you'll rehearse the creak and shuffle of the stages of your life
till you hear the tears that start at the recall
and the flushing of the blood at the remembering
of the feats, humiliations, joys, defeats, applause . . .

when familiar with the motions and emotions of a life
you have ears for the inaudible
whispering you to act.

New Name and Blessing

She holds her breath, sitting under green water,
fearful to breathe, especially breathe what looks
sedate indoors, as if in captivity brooks
turn grave and sink. On rocks they spray her to laughter.
She sinks, supported by Grampa, who bathes her a Latter-
day Saint in an echoing font awash among bricks,
and rises into the prayer that has echoed to fix
her name in birth: Meadow, Jesus's daughter.

Confirming her choice of new father, her father's breath
calls for the burning of spirit to light and to dry her,
warming the assembly of saints, as her baptism chilled
him, and a few family friends, witnessing death —
on her he calls a blessing down the stilled
attention held like tinder for the fire.

Ramses II

for Clinton F. Larson

How time permutes all glory! Ramses, now —
who confiscated temples and monuments
others had started; who, in his name's defense,
ordered it cut where he had chiseled out
the names of others — he at the end got down
to temples to the day of his birth, immense
quivers hewn to level the day's intense
shaft of dawn full on his form cut in stone.

Ramses is now a contraceptive jelly,
his temples at Abu Simbel artful fakes
jacked high above the lake Nasser decreed
and Krushchev filled — so high, in fact, it takes
an extra day for probing dawn to speed
those hundred sixty feet and strike his belly.

On the Stranding of Great Whales

They come to the beach for the reasons we take the sand:
to hear the ocean polishing off the earth,
show off, whistle, beachcomb, display their girth,
and watch the water shelve off into land.

Or grounded even for frolicking with their food—
or something mundane; not running before the wind
to find calm harbor, nor trying to breathe in
freshets to clear the blow-hole of freakish spume.

Not instinct herding them after a dying leader,
not trapped by the ebb while feeding on herring shoals,
nor running aground while fleeing attacking sharks,
nor misdirected by parasites in their ears.

They come to smell wild roses beyond the sand,
to see the green of anything growing but kelp,
to hear their whistles and grunts echo off cliffs,
the cries they hurl, sounding for something unsound.

Searching for Tethys and the shallow, tepid water
where Pakicetus took it into his head
to dive a little, hunting a larger cod,
they come to the beach for the same reason we go there:

to see the great mother.

CLIFTON JOLLEY

Prophet

". . . no beauty that we should desire him."
ISAIAH 53:2

The common cripple to the south of Palmyra
Dreamed God the Father, the Savior Son,
And, though clerical tradition predetermine his doom,
Can never, never, never
Search Kidd's treasure again.

Stout, paunched, hook-nosed mystic though he was —
Who gimped his way from fourteen on
Through the dark, deep furrows of those New York farms
To Ohio, Missouri, Illinois (and beyond) —
He faced Gethsemane alone,
Crossed back from deliverance,
And, from an upper room above the crowds
Who shouted blood upon their children's heads,
Reached wide his trembling hands to God,
Was pierced,
And, plunging headlong into Pentecost,
Was dead.

Mr. Bojangles

Bojangles so much burdens me
With his memory
That I am often caught, mid syllable,
As he stitches back the grey fields of my brain —
Hems my seldom freedom
With the snipping clip and canter
Of his heels
And toe-down spin that pins me to his pain.

"I read in the *Daily Herald*
That some negras east of here
Went wild and killed . . . "

The impossibly mad and running rhythms of your soul
Were all you needed then.
How many butlers had you played?
How many times the fool?
How many county fairs
The accolade of time must count you for?

Beneath the door
I see your shadow skipping, skipping, skipping
Along the light
And wonder that those years pursuing
Brought you little further on or more
Than they pursued against the night.

But we are free men now, then, old man.
Our names are James, and George, and Mister,
Who see you from a wall bestride the years
As you flicker . . .
        As you flicker . . .
                As you flicker . . .

Shirley Temple has grown from plump to fat,
And old Bojangles,
Sole worn through behind the tap,
From black to Black.

ANITA TANNER

Residual Farmer

The only man around who lives inside
the house where he was born. His sons are gone,
care little for the farm because he saw
them educated well, not satisfied
with what the family farm could give. Upon
his land through void of time he's set his jaw
against the subsidies — the only flaw
in farming, that it's obsolete. Each dawn,
slant afternoon, a little stooped, he leans
toward his chores with crinkled eyes and yawns
into the sun, his farm a remnant pride
from horse-drawn mower to his new machines
that link him to the soil, to all that greens
beneath his rubber boots, his slowing stride.

Finding Questions

Rummaging through old books,
kneeling against ancestral trunks,
although you've scavenged here so many times,
you find them, this time, new.

Pages crackle from an old King James
as if they've grown together
in the dark of attic.
All your life you've heard these verses,
taken them as gospel—
now they somehow change.

It could be the mellow light of the setting sun
through an attic window
or the odor of moth balls and dust
that distends your nostrils in the heat,
but from your own hands cradling
the cracked leather binding,

as if for the first time, you suddenly sense
beneath the transparent skin of your knuckles
what must be miles and miles of veins.

KATHY EVANS

Handwritten Psalm
for my father

Certain the ashes
found wings

like those small birds
taking flight

over water,
I think about

the heart,
how it rises

in its dark cavity
for the last time

and this pattern
of birds, strangely

perfect
against the sky.

Midnight Reassembled

Tonight the stars
are as inaudible as stones
in water, and the moon
hangs there spare
telling us nothing of our place
in this universe. Night builds
over us like a hut,
a thin defense.
I lift the child's head
as if it were a molecule
I'll come to love.
Somewhere, out there
in the immensity of night
a swan glides across
the surface of its own image,
wings touching wings on the water.
We touch the world this way.
The stars fall dumb,
the moon a feather, a life
drifts to the other side of the pond.
It's what the Japanese once called
a slender sadness.

Bright Waves and Separate Entities

A fleet of schooners leaves me beached.
No sand. My legs swing wide. Water.
Salt. Brine. Gulls tumble in air.
They circle in gowns. The only light
is the white light of their wings.
There are four stars over me.
She is one of them. She falls,
plunges, then like a small diver
surfacing for air, emerges, head first,
skin slick. She slides out into their hands,
cold star-child, born, lovelier
than the pond newt I held one morning in May;
more beautiful than my father swimming
in a bay of stinging jelly-fish. My head
is a loft of bells, clanging out of sequence
and I hear eight million peasants cheer
this infant, breathing inside her satin skin,
crying "World! World!" to the midnight gulls.

Red

The softest part is the entrance. Slide
sideways under the exit sign. It's not
just a few tomatoes splitting on a vine,
Cadillacs and hot peppers, but lip pulp
and neon. You can still see it when
the lights short out, pulsing. It's not
just a laminated fingernail, nor veins
at intersections in the eye, not a reflex,
not a skid. It's the heart pumping against
conclusions; the heart attempting its second
dive. More than the brand iron searing the side
of the Angus, not the Fourth of July streamer,
but the nipple after sex, holly berry in the rain,
not a barn, but a scream, the lobster hissing,
a tulip, the positive part of the wing.

Half the Ferris Wheel

for my father

If ever you belonged back in this world,
it is tonight — streets full of stray dogs,
insects in orchestra. You send down stars,
falling along my arms like birthmarks.
Who rides on the black rim of the telescope?
I've climbed this hill to look at the comet,
but it's only the moon I see, half
the ferris wheel. You are up there on top.
The seats rock back and forth in the wind.

STEVEN WILLIAM GRAVES

Hard Freight

Against the eastern bench where foothills
shelve, homes, homes squared and roofed
with earth-toned tiles or fat, wood shakes
to keep late rain light banter
or wind-whipped snow a muffled bark,
to maintain a civil distance
between the civil disobedience
of the out-of-doors and us.

This year precautions seem
unfounded. We have had
such a mild start to winter,
mid-December and mere bright braids of snow
to lace the more protected flanks
of the higher nearby peaks.
Inside, in the cool, dry cellar
the pale yellow apples pulled down
this autumn sit in gunny sacks
or bushel baskets. The apricots
are paraffined in bottles and jars—
fruits we've grown and gathered from the orchard
planted long before, and set below.

And yet within this house's shelter,
despite the tempered weather,
the night has tampered with my son's sleep,
menacing him with a cold,
unseen noise. I try to reassure him
it is only a late train whose cars
force their weight upon the same raw joints
of rail placed halfway through the valley,
whose severed whistling is sent to stir
the unprepared station or hail
a one-width slip of road it will cross.

Finally, after whispered comforts
my son resumes his sleep, but truthfully
I have given him half answers
not mentioning the harbinger
of hard freight, for the startled rails
set forth again that bold dare you too will face,
that pull you cannot easily unfreight
that draws one from the trailer court or farm
or even nestled home up the canyon
beneath the pre-dawn sky with promises.
And so we may become rolling stock, jarred
and wrenched into a home-sliding wind
on which we send back faintly
and then more faintly, now but then
at ever longer interval
our vow one day to return.

The Cancellation

Men less sensitive have struggled with this:
the breach in which our lives are tailored
for disappointment: the long wait in queues
as the drama is sold out. We ponder
our calendars and are troubled. We will
stand in countless scenes at piers and platforms
paying homage to the receding face,
the small receding face. Days after, walking
to the market or mornings in the gray office
we will rethink our multiple replies.
We will rehearse a more sufficient speech
for strangers, for friends become strangers.

The Dunes at Truro

1.

It seemed that everyone ached to eat fried clams.
Brokers stuck in offices bitched and whined.
In bottlenecks that straddled frequent woods
the air was hard to swallow and everywhere
the amplified chirr of bugs jarred.
At noon the horizon sent up a trial-
balloon-sized cloud which grew so blue
we only supposed we saw it pass.
We were deep enroute when the expletives
of gulls played above the black butter of road.
Only then the nudge of air reeked kelp
as it had reeked lacquer, vinyl, blistered tires.
A corridor of stunted scrub gave out
at a fenced plateau and the innuendo of the sea.
And the cantilevered mist hammered overhead
like birds unnested by the mildly fractious waves
hung in heat paralysis. Our feet were harmed
first with incandescent sand then pained
by ocean swirl. About us the coast stood
replete in mounds of dazzled quartz
though we saw only women, contoured
with expectation, hinged in lime green suits.

2.

The tongue that finagler has stumbled upon
salt. A summer's worth of heat-charged ocean air
alights now during days of cooler weather.
The spring-laid shingles, once blond and confluent
are gray, streaked, and slightly withdrawn. Rain moves
the salt within their skins as well as off,
pickling woodstuffs. The tongue makes one of its four
pronouncements of taste, and inside the porch
with its jalousied windows for a season
salt is held to be domesticated.

3.

Equinox. Against the doors of neighbors
still here, votive maize, as if one grew
autumn leaves from bad teeth. Clairvoyance.
The late afternoon sun standing in shallow
pools of toppled daiquiris atop the dunes
at Truro. The sands bronzed. The overhead
pale, beset with clouds that wheel and fold
in light diluted much with cold vast gulfs
of air. The cottages repeat themselves
along the bay like lavishly made up dolls
left behind like seasonal friends, amid
lost souvenirs, those cheerless, forearm-length
fish which seasonly succumb in rows that mark
the last high tide. The alliances of birds
retracing the broad Gulf Stream. Weatherizing.
Laying in wood against our nearing
uncertainties. Reckoning human chill
in cords and calling our feckless thoughts
back from their scalloped steps along the dunes.

4.

At noon the wind gave out its siren sound
and sullen forces swept across the headlands
of the Cape and moved inland. Quickly
the tiny corridors of roads were filled
with anxious traffic and so too, quickly clogged.
Finally, we were on foot, our movements
miscued: hilarious pratfalls, arabesques.
But the snow came harder, horizontal,
uncontrolled until the lights of Wellfleet
were extinguished. We took our bearings
from abandoned cars perilously spaced,
pointing wherever their spins had come
to stand. The bitter air took up the sea
at land's end and shattered the great bar
at Chatham, flooding the darkened land
with darkened brine. Even our own limbs had grown
remote. We feared our body's weight. Some sat

upon the sand whom we forced to stand again.
From the distant overhead in the voices
of the drowned, something like our names
was roared and roared. The snowfall choked
the dunes at Truro, snows thick
to their being black, hissing at our knees.

Early Invitations

Come with me. Let us begin by setting
off at day among ragged blue haystacks
and rods of sun disciplining ice-green
fields, the nearest neighbor's first (a quiet
stand of cottonwoods shielding ours). Begin
moving to the applause of bells, still out

of sight, carillons carried by wind out
of the mouth of cowbells, the cows setting
off themselves because of day. Let us begin
in the new-mown fields and cone-shaped haystacks
erupting from the field's breadth where quiet
birds, intensely black, strut across the green.

Then dawn's fire spills across as well, parts green
from green: three greens and brass exploding out
of the applauding cottonwoods toward quiet
birds feeding unaware. The fields' setting,
ribbed and ribboned with half-purple haystacks
and their deeply purpled shadows, begins

in cottonwood and ends in sound, begins
and begins again in bells and wind-green
mimicry of flight, the haystacks'
locust-dazed note, katydids calling out
from cottonwood, the farmboy's cry setting
bells on edge: simpler songs. The long-quiet

birds refuse the earth, and the once-quiet
field brims with ascending applause, begins
in applause and ends in music. Setting
off across an ordered earth, brass and green,
the farmboy plays with air, airs, and flight, out-
singing birds and the now whiffling haystacks,

whistling with the winnowing of haystacks.
Musicians herd in the dispelled quiet,
tolling through the cottonwoods, sounding out
cadence, cadenza. And the woods begin
with light from the white undersides of green
laughter, to welcome us to this setting.

Setting out in the quiet of the day,
our vision of haystacks and birds begins
in blue and ends in sounds intensely green.

RANDALL L. HALL

Brazilian Afternoons

On verandas, in the arbored shade of vines and trees,
The old men sit
With spittle and the stain of *maté*
Drying in their beards.
The afternoon wraps all around them
Like melting folds of fine, hot gauze
New woven by the bold Brazilian sun.

The skin upon their dwindling bodies
Has receded in the tide of age.
Their voices are remote.
Their sentences emerge at crippled intervals,
So oddly timed.

They are a double circle
With the passing of a hollowed gourd
That holds the broken, benedictory leaves of tea
And steaming water.

Their deliberate ripeness set beyond us
Waiting
Waiting in the melting gauze of summer afternoons.

The Apogee of Loneliness

On the lake
A few ducks drift among the shallows.

A muskrat, frightened,
Draws his robe of wrinkled water
Toward the far shore and the final hush of light.

Cautiously we move toward the water's edge.
The sound of stone on stone
Goes quickly out across the water,
Ringing flatly past the hills
For as far as sound will go.

We watch the wind-led waves roll ineluctably away

And listen as
The thin-split voice of many birds
Evaporates into the skies.

The pressure of your hand upon my arm surprises me,
Coming, as it does, from farther
Than the fragile light of stars

For we have reached the apogee of loneliness,
Curving on the farthest edge of autumn,
So near escaping from the reassurance of return
We hold our breath.

Passover: A Mirrored Epiphany

How many years from Bethlehem
Until the awful eloquence
Of wine and lamb
And bitter herbs
Took his breath,
Stunned Him suddenly with knowledge,

Revealing that the blood
Once painted on the lintels and the door posts
Was his own

And the slain lamb but his shadow and a mirror?

In that moment, bitter herbs,
Dissolving slowly on his tongue,
Insinuated such enormous grief a shudder split his heart
And plumbed towards eternity

Where all night he lay in wonder
In the center of a hundred billion stars,
Tugged and beckoned by the nascent possibilities
Of love or abdication.

Winter Landscape

The frigid hills, bound silently in snow,
Hunch together, hurting in the brittle freeze.

The stream is glazed with ice,
Chilled to silence;
What has not frozen struggles
Among the rounded stones.

The fragile sky,
Stretched tight and thin as blue can be,
Is just degrees from shattering like glass.

The cold has swallowed all the movement,
All the sound,
And now surrounds us,
Eager for our breath.

Suddenly, a yellow bird no bigger than my heart
Flits overhead like one quick pulse of light.

A small warmth in a shiver of space.

LINDA SILLITOE

The Old Philosopher

It is worth the coin in pain to wrench my head,
confronting the repeated noise of bird
that interrupts internal tedium.
There. Upon that slanting post a red
smudge between dark wings, a robin's word
to anyone, "here I am, I am,"

is the second thing I like. The first is this:
my cell is three doors past the delivery room
and every child drenched in sudden air
who finds his toes unraveled from his hair
hands flapping no boundaries, the womb
well lost, wails his knowledge, I exist!

> *My numbed and stricken wife, for my pleading*
> *blinked one eye to affirm identity*
> *true as one Indian intricately beading*
> *a bricklayer slapping strophe after strophe*
> *like a typewriter bleed blow breath*
> *build brick whack blood death*

> These thoughts unlatch the joinings of the walls
> which float away. The sounds of bird and squalling
> infant keen the idiom of skies—
> not of stars, but of unseen thinkers differing
> as star from star. One like a comet falls
> in wingless flight, a newborn human cries.

> My voice is mine, my hands grope loosening air,
> within my brain a heart, within an ear
> that hears another voice. Know that I
> am Alpha and Omega, Lord of sky
> and earth, beginning and end, exalt and damn.

> *The robin spoke the word: Ego, I am.*

an early elegy in lower case

i pay my respects by saying what's true
    in love and anger

you served us crumbs, you see, and we hungered
    for our own bowls
    of bread and milk

love your silvery chains, my sisters
    we did   we do
for they are your redemption

oh it is not so simple says my brain
    he let sisters too
gowned in white into those clean chambers

american brothers too are yoked unequally

but it is too late now for anything
but the oversimplification from my heart

in this lush room where we keep prophet ghosts
    i want to fold you in
like a child too sleepy to trust in slumber

but say instead goodbye   hopeflicker   goodbye

for my brothers' sake I weep at your death
for my sisters i keep my seat as you pass

Song of Creation

Who made the world, my child?
    Father made the rain
    silver and forever.
        Mother's hand
drew riverbeds and hollowed seas,
drew riverbeds and hollowed seas
    to bring the rain home.

Father bridled winds, my child,
    to keep the world new.
        Mother clashed
fire free from stones
and breathed it strong and dancing,
and breathed it strong and dancing
    the color of her hair.

He armed the thunderclouds
    rolled out of heaven;
    Her fingers flickered
        hummingbirds
weaving the delicate white snow,
weaving the delicate white snow
    a waterfall of flowers.

And if you live long, my child,
    you'll see snow burst
        from thunderclouds
    and lightning in the snow;
listen to Mother and Father laughing,
listen to Mother and Father laughing
    behind the locked door.

Some Nights

Some nights in a small cove
sea and shore talk endlessly
(of dapples shallows hollows)
seeking sun despite the polar
breath from dark's yawning throat

Some nights we hear crickets
(never sleep never sleep
beneath warm moonwashed trees)
composing old impromptu music
with silent mouths and singing limbs

Impossibly other nights
crickets sing in that crack
where sea answers shore
violining melodies pitched
between the currents of our speech

A Lullaby in the New Year

One week is not too soon to learn a very
early language; for your spine to be aware
that a rocking chair means comfort and your wary
nerves want sleep. Nothing will disappear,
forsaking you to vast, fluorescent air
your fists and feet can't pummel. You shudder
at my kiss, a random bother in your hair.
I tell you this, my loud and little daughter,
you have now all there is: familiar dark,
a blanket's wings without, warm milk within,
balanced with your head in my hand's cup
in a second cradle of flesh and sound. We rock
and still you rage. I kiss your hair again.
All right, I whisper, accept, accept and sleep.

Missing Persons

I know where the bodies are buried
in my house and can whistle past
indefinitely before I must dig and sift.

Almost at once, the remains of a girl scout
at nine, her green uniform folded more neatly
than it was worn, the sturdy body quite gone.

A turquoise bib recalls the chubby boy
with oatmeal around the mouth that opened,
swallowed, despite the sound asleep eyes.

Lost her baby, I heard then, in between
those I kept; only to find the more
they survive, the more I lose them again.

What do I do now with this doll dress
my lastborn wore for ten miniature months?

How do I greet these ghosts who haunt
the remains of the children? The young
mother who dressed each child in red

for this photo? The weary one who rocked
until dawn? The yellowed newspaper girl
smiling like a bride? Under the most dust

I find the diary kept from twelve to sixteen,
about boys, often as not, keening for them
as if nothing mattered but scouting out love.

There is nothing here I can keep or discard.
I'm putting it all back, sprinkling dust
over the top and closing the closet door

as if, in the dark, the ghosts will rest.

During Recess

As court's proceeded, spring has come.
One noon, I walk from my office to my old
neighborhood and find it well-kept.
The ditch I'd hurtle galloping home
from school has been curbed and guttered.

Jack's shop is run by Asians now
who mop, exchanging Vietnamese. I buy candy
from the uncrowded shelves and turn toward work
tracing the old route to junior high.
Behind me, my elementary school hollers its recess.

Listening back, I hear my own voice, my own
shoes on the hopscotch, swiftly recalling how
to ignore the bell until the line forms
then beat the blood in my face to the door
where I assume that Miss Blunt still waits.

No one supposes I am walking back to my ugly notes
on a double murder, a naturalist losing spring
to unearth a spider web. Extricated, it must gleam
geometrically, word by word. Sunstreams, continue your
hard green in the surprised leaves; give me, unjustified,

what killing cost: more sky, more time.

Killer

Sometime before it became too late
you should have been brought here
and doused in red and blue
(some green)
until your inky caverns emptied
poison on the red clay
and left you whole.

Poison to be powdered
like burned bone
under the Navajo sun
then swept on a long tangent
by the dark wind.
nor could you approach
this land unrecognized: here

a sane man lives by his heart.
a crazy man lives in his head.

Letter to a four-year-old daughter

The days you instill in me only exhaustion,
reverberating from living room walls,
leaping, hanging, hurling as you instruct,
"Listen but don't look — tell me what this hits!"
I force my eyes to look calmly at a coloring book,
stained-glass with fifty colors patched on a waxy duck,

and send you off to sing, riding breakneck
on your toy horse to rhythms of "I am a child
of God," leaving me penitent in my fatigue.
As you compose, "Joseph Smith was a good prophet . . . "
I recall with renewal the day at your insistence
you learned how he was murdered. Refusing evasion,

you required whole truth, scorning attempts
at explanation, tolerance, and a happy ending
in heaven; you choked down scrambled eggs, weeping,
"But they didn't have to kill him," and again
at bedtime, "they didn't have to kill him."
Like Porter Rockwell, one of few, you inquired,

"Who were they, what were their names?"
Now, horse providing percussion, you end your song,
"It was so long ago, we don't know their names,
don't know their names." In a sudden double-exposure
I glimpse a hounded man — a prophet — and a blond head
bowed for blood that shines from a newly found grave.

SUSAN HOWE

Summer days, a Painting by Georgia O'Keeffe

The skull of an elk is the center — parched, cleaned
Of flesh, whorls of brown and white space
Where eyes and nostrils used to be.
Three-pronged antlers curl out of the head
Like our best thoughts, pointing out
Where things are and what we do
And do not know. The skull floats in the vacant
Sky, a mirage as deep as life, antlers
Earth-brown, darker along the curves.

The skull broods over the living
Flowers, the rest of the mirage, bright desert
Blossoms of yellow, red, mauve. Sturdy and
Delicate, they pull us in like a heart
Beat, like love. Pull us as far as we can go.

Behind the skull and the flowers, the horizon
Marks the limits. Hot sandstone mountains
Range under a sea of clouds as here and there the sky
Pools. We want to see forever into
Summer, but boundaries hold.
Brought back to the center, we belong
To the mirage: Above a brief flowering
Heart, behind our own faces, we feel
Eyeless sockets and the silent, imminent skull.

To my Great-great Grandmother, Written on a Flight to Salt Lake City

Caught here, in an arc
Between the sea coast where your ocean
Voyage left you, and the mountains
Where you walked to make your home,
I see, at last, grandmother
Of my grandmother, you whom I have never known.

It is the light. Flying westward
In a craft of air holds darkness off.
It has been sunset for a long time.
Hours stretch in a thin curve, arcing
Back before flight, before the sun
Caught vapor trails across the sky.

You were the one who walked this route
Seven miles below, stone-cut
Feet seeking sand or turf to ease
The stiffness — and your arms, thin,
Spare from pulling all your earthly
Goods behind. You were almost lost

Within those miles where the earth curves
Away from me, but a stream of light
Burned — and when I looked away, there
You were. Perhaps because the legacy
You offered me finds symbol in the place
To which I journey as deliberately

As you walked. Or because at the end
Of every seven-, ten-, or fifteen-mile day,
You stood, just at sunset, squinting at the golden
Dust of those who walked ahead, sure that your journey
Would endure. You saw then the burning
Through which I see you. Sunlight where we both dwell.

Things in the Night Sky

First the deepening of elements we long for
Like myth, forgiving experience into patterns
We can scatter, random as stars.
The call of a bird lifts its own coolness,
Music like *weep* and *few*. Bats awaken, fly.
The vast, hollow dome evening is becoming
Reminds us we live on a planet and can endure
Absence, where we're moving,
Though not without incidents
Of light. Intent, we study darkness
To learn metaphors for light.

We have always imposed ourselves
Upon the sky. We say *darkness grows
Or gathers*, as if it were a crop,
Name planets for ourselves, our gods.
And through the night, draw lines
That aren't there, connect stars
Into semblances we can survive—Lion, Hunter, Swan.
But stars, immense, burn and burn
And luminous galaxies spiral
Beyond our planet's small noise.
Their gravity would call us out.
We are surrounded by ancient light
We can't see, come millions of years
Through space we can't recite.

When things in the night sky
Impose themselves on us, imprint
Their being into our slim hearts,
We might approach our work of becoming.
Sight will exceed density,
And we'll rise beyond Earth,
Beyond our own names,
Receiving infinite differences,
Dark centers of bright stars.

The Woman Whose Brooch I Stole

She hadn't hoped to be lifted through herself,
Slip in gaudy moments
Beyond her own grave. A niece and nephew
Came to make sure she wouldn't,
Stuffing the dumpster with layers of her life.
But the jewelry was there, beneath the plastic
And lace existence they threw out and I found,
Rummaging down to the time
Her name was Mabel and she liked to bowl,
Crocheted doilies covered frayed arms
Of her overstuffed chairs, and she accepted gifts
She'd never use — stationery and boxed soap.
I didn't take it all, just earrings,
Silver with blue stones, cat's-eye green,
And the pair to match the brooch,
Glorious bauble, and I wear it
To see her, fierce behind the pin,
Coming through in pink glitter and gold.

MARY BLANCHARD

Elegy for Geoffrey Barber

we are still driving away
from the cemetery stunned
by your leaving, half expecting
to see your bright face;
a little boy's ineffable sweetness
no under-the-counter prescription
could ever replace.
we see you, each in his own way,
knowing we have not healed completely
because we still need you, Geoffrey.
when we lock the screen doors
at night against the burglars and
the apocalypse we are saying
our memories of you will turn us slowly
into who we really are.
we will go back and back to the day
when you said good-bye
until we see your face again
and our doors are unlocked forever

Prayers

for Sylvia Plath

Even God is an atheist, but
sometimes at dusk he glides down
through vacuous black, hovers
over the world searching for something
lost—time, or truth maybe?
In low tones he chants garbled prayers
to little girls, kneeling by their beds.
Someone whispers: help me,
show me the way . . . he knows he can never
show his face. No one ever hears him.
In a vase on the kitchen table
limp orchids die slowly in darkness,
their pale moist lips open, straining
as if to scream.

Bereft

the man who lives behind us
whose fence we share
the one whose wife left
suddenly last may
has let his fruit trees go
wild and unpruned, heavy with
fat ripe plums and golden apricots
that hang way over
our side of the fence, reaching arms
full and wild with leaves
bent down with so much fruit
it spills torn, oozing-sweet
onto our lawn

Liar

I love your lies
they are so transparent
and convincing

carefully wrapped
handed to me like a package
of hotdogs exposed

in neat obscene little
exhibitionist rows
next to the bologna

when I bite into
one of them it tastes
like boeuf bouillabaisse

because I know
the difference
between true lies and
lies that are true

ROB HOLLIS MILLER

For Kathleen

—marriage—

memory won't fade with seasons

like voices in the wind, heard
clear for miles

(winter winds
rage in trees

but turn playful in spring
caress twigs to bloom
and summer green

in autumn winds
and leaves
discuss Glories)

eventually intelligible

mythical bird

the hollering and
beating of bushes by
the older scouts decreases
recedes
and finally ceases

the Tenderfoot
crouches holding
a paper bag
his thighs
ache   slight
wind rustling of branches
and something
a leaf or
mouse maybe
nibbling along the ground
dont impinge on the
silence
enclosing him

the stars
bright as newly created

flashes in his eyes
scurry like birds
across the
dark grass

in a half hour
(yuga)
he realizes
there is
no
such thing as a snipe
and he will have
to make his way
back
to the campfire
alone afraid
of the night
he doesnt think to leave the empty bag

the snipe oblivious to ritual
goes on year after
year
mating rearing young nesting
pecking around scurrying out of the way
oblivious to evolution

The Law of Gravity

This man, my grandfather,
once as solid and permanent
as Ruby Peak,
I recognize now only by his rocking chair
and laugh.

His body flutters around him nearly free of gravity.

I try to imagine his laugh
dispersing too
as I tried at six to imagine
myself buried, in a kind of night, sleep, a dark
buried, held down by dirt, dead . . .
I scared myself.

Scared again I wish the valley
would collapse in protest:
The Wallowa Mountains bury all;

Accept the data:
the wind in the curtains
flutters
like butterflies.

M. D. PALMER

First Spring

The first spring after the fall
We married, things kept coming up
Around our house in ways
I had not noticed before.
Like bulbs, grape hyacinth first
Then the daffodils and crocus,
Thick green tips coming up
Clean through the soft mud.
We cleared away the grasses
And weeds to give them the room
They seemed to want to grow.
We did it several times.
Once on Sunday morning
We cleared out a place
Below our bedroom window.
The footings of the house
Were large sharp grey stones
Not cut or faced or even set
With mortar. They had been
Roughly mated and remained
Still solid in spite of
Ninety winters and their
Substantial eccentricities.
The flowers seemed to know that
Bed below the stones and grew
There all that spring. And we
Admired what seemed to be an
Old arrangement as we worked
Together toward a rhythm of our own.

Rural Tortillas

Out in the country
things seemed to change.
The cobblestone streets
became open spaces
between trees and vines.
The bus to the country
was like a caterpillar
halfway changed to butterfly,
the bottom was a flat bed truck
above the wheels were
open buckboard benches and
a canopy with scalloped
edges. There was no aisle
and the fare taker worked
his way from front to back
juggling change and hanging
onto the outside like someone
from a circus as we bounced
along over the mud holes.

In the country, the tortillas
were all hand work, first
in the wrists, rocking the
hand stone over the flat stone,
each movement catching
a few more kernels, like
the old shell and pea game,
a mesmerizing rhythm
now you see them
now you don't,
then the palm and finger work,
the round dough ball
with only some quick patting
becoming thin and circular,
resting lightly over the back
of the hand like a magic
handkerchief, and last
the griddle, a piece of
steel with a little curve to it,
maybe a part of a truck hood,
perhaps a Ford that had started
in Detroit and worked its
way south as it got older,
but here all traces of
its former life were gone. Here
above the fire things were
changed. Here the tortilla,
with a pinch of salt,
grasped flat between two
hands, like applause
or prayer, was rolled to be eaten.
The mother pinched two
ears in the soft dough
and called it a little burro,
and the child smiled one
more time at their old joke.

After Thunder

This creek is singing the song that
comes after thunder, tumbling small
stones together till they are smooth

as eggs, opening around an upright
twig, rubbing its sides and making
it quiver and coming together again

after, combing green tangles of water
grass over a place where two legs of
the stream meet after opening around

a log. This is the blood of the earth,
clear and moving always toward the
deeper places, hurrying always in and

down, giving and taking as pattern
the movement of time through the
mind and the gray of age through the

body. Some will give itself to roots
and leave the wheel of births as
the small breaths of forest leaves in

the sun. Some will become as salty
as tears, resting in deeps still except
to brush along hard scales and cold

wide eyes. And some will find itself
lifted up and drawn by light and wind,
taken lightly from the tips of waves

and passed, breeze by breeze to high
cold places, almost above the thunder
but not beyond what pulls us down and in.

Coda

After the crowning moment,
the entrances and ovations,
I saw, in a pause,
as if for the first time,
the doctor working quietly.
It was three a.m. and
his shoelaces were loose,
his sleep and dreams
were somewhere else,
his eyes full and distinct
in the strong light,
his fingers moving
from habit to skill
and from skill to grace,
crouching there on a low stool
like a tailor
matching a complex tweed,
or a gardener
smoothing back
the soil disturbed in harvest.

STEPHEN ORSON TAYLOR

A Faun, on Reading Horace's Address
to the Spring of Bandusia

There is no answer to the flow of swift water;
As it moves, white or still on the surface,
Deep water drifts through stone or moss with the same insistence
Planets circle the sun,
Or stars pursue their more intricate courses:
Nothing marks the center of that movement, but

The pattern of the dance

A spring or star may mock an eye not practiced in their motion,
Which defines the difference between an ancient poem
And the spring it praised (the quick water born there,
For the moment, for the ear and the eye,
Prattling wisdom or nonsense,
Leaps over the stones; the poet
Addled with the brightness of the sunlight,
Cannot name the least of its whorls):

Old Horace, fool, watched it vanish
And caught no trace of its going,
Though every atom ran the length of the stream bed,
Or seeping through the gates of sandstone,
Sought the dark seas of the earth's still depths,
Or blowing into mist at the stone's edge,

Drifted in the sun's heat,
And at night descended on the quiet grass
To glitter in the last starlight, and chill my feet.

The Love of Christ, and Spring

Christmas past and the advent of small birds come,
Delighting in nothing but dried seeds
With paper wings wind-torn beyond flight,

Sad King David finds new love: a maiden mistress,
To lend his old flesh heat,
Makes ruddy flowers blossom in his cheek.

No more backing up to fires; the king will burn within
Though winter sheet the earth in ice
And fill the wind with sleet.

Whatever dead Chaldeans say
Who read Egyptian books and struggled with the universe
To number years and days,

Whatever the precise angle light defines at noon
Above the southern ridge,
Or whatever stands of pine may shield

The entrances and exits of the sun and moon,
Or through whatever track of night
The Swan flies north by darkened ways,

Whether rising moon or setting sun
Make pale our vision of her grace,
To bring her gifts to wise men, fools beyond hope,

That lady follows star-winds
Although they be so cold
Her breath streams back a mist of ice, among the stars a road.

Sophia

I searched that old house for you,
Opening the doors of closed rooms,
Asking the curtains and the chairs,
"Is she here?"

They answered in their silence,
"No, she is not; no, she is not,"
Though a hand had opened the curtain
For sunlight,

And left the chairs misarranged at the hearth,
Fire dark upon the stone:
Someone had come before me,
Here or there touched something,

And left a fire, now grey ash.
I could look for nothing definite,
A sudden shift of light or shade
Not quite the sun's,

Hoping the image of some object
Would resolve in a vision of meaning;
Then I would leave,
Closing that door behind me.

One might pass down the long corridors
And for their subtle curves
Never come to the same room,
That door never looked for

Which would open to my touch,
Leaving still the question of the presence
Which had placed an object
So the sunlight,

Coming through the window,
Would refract its color
Into some darker corner,
Or, caught in a crystal on the sill,

Unfold my sight in fire,
Or draw my vision beyond,
Beyond the window
And across the lawn,

Over the green hedge
To the lake,
Smooth grey at dawn, fire at sunset,
Or blue in the hot noon, nearly as dark as when,

At evening, Mercury or Venus
Could be seen, reflected
Near the pale curve of the new moon,
But never, for all that,

An answer to my question.

On the Evening of President Smith's Leaving

To watch the sunset
We climbed into the hills,
But the sun looked as if it might go down
In shifts from blue, to grey, to darkness,
And leave the valley to watch bright stars made dim with Sabbath smoke.
However, at sunset the wind came up and blew in thin ice clouds,
Dust over the western hills from the deserts beyond Moab,
Bringing sage, spice, cinnamon, cedar oil
In long processions like the ones which carried
Jacob Israel, Mother Sarah, Father Joseph home,
Ruddy gold over the salt wastes,
Desolate places to be crossed;
But the sky was filled with trains of red
Darkened only to more royal and more somber scarlet,
Purple of the King of only kings of kings,
And we cannot say we wept with only sadness,
That our tears came but of grief.

RICHARD TICE

Fly Fishing

Like a dry fly, feathered and barbed,
cast into air farther and farther,
setting a zigzag of red and black
on the extremity of green
undulating line, threading
shadows and first light:

As if a mimetic insect in the S
of flight dips suddenly to fleck
the dark, intimating pool,
rimmed by shore and roiling water,
and rest, circle centered,
before its first, convulsive throe:

Some words suggestive of meaning, tossed
to what has only been a guess
lurking by submerged rock, that lure —
to break surface in explosion —
a sleek sinuous upward arching
gleaming rainbow of perception.

Decision

Dawn, and you walk the street again
apart from younger friends who come
uncalled to windows, wondering
what you could feel each morning there.
You've talked enough of eighty years
to guess. There's something about streets
less limited than walls on days
that threaten to repeat, the choice
each day between the narrowing
of walls or narrowing of world.

Into light

The sand, white as salt
and sunlight, is whiter
than seagulls, than wind
whitening the waves, is higher

than seagulls' cries,
rises beyond the sounding
whitecaps and climbs
to a silent sky losing

all its whiteness to where
the sand peaks, then masses
for the final, heavy curve
hurling from sight into forever.

Haiku

the persimmon leaf
follows a different path down
than the one before

night in the sickroom
the throbbing of my temple
and the crickets cry

night rain
against the water, young rice
into the rain

now the wild geese
now the far-off child
call and call

KAREN MARGUERITE MOLONEY

Relinquishing

We didn't know how softly you would die,
Who might have bled at any orifice.
You simply loosed a final, shallow sigh.
Your cheek is chill, but dry beneath my kiss.

Already cold, the quiet body lies,
The ravage done, small protest to the sheet.
Beyond the window through November skies,
Sycamore leaves go drifting to the street.

The nurses in the hallway, speaking low,
Are waiting now, impatient to proceed.
The yellow leaves are noiseless as they go,
But fall so easily — and gather speed.

Snowfall on Glenflesk

The hush that sheathes the road is sure and slow.
My lights suspend a galaxy of flakes:
The silence is as haunted as the snow.

I conjure kindred names I would not know
Had no one told me how your welcome wakes
The hush around your turf-fire, sure and slow;

Had Conor and his liegemen long ago
Been late to flock the glen beyond the lakes,
Their sanctum still as haunted as the snow;

Or had you never dusted off to show
The pedigrees you walked these hills to make.
The hush that sheathes the farm is sure and slow,

And still you jigsaw all the leads I know,
Till, dancing down the fields of my mistakes,
The sentence comes as swiftly as the snow:

"Curreal! Your Julia's from Curreal. And so
It seems you're kin to half the valley's folks."
The hush that sheathes the glen is sure and slow,
Our sanctum still as haunted as the snow.

The Truant Officer Recalls Sweet Maggie

Loved her? I left her. Don't think that qualifies.
She's single still (you know the grapevine here),
And back in school. *That* came as no surprise:
An ace brain, the safety there, her fear of getting stuck

Slaving away with the rest of us peons —
The job for her a chance to save some bucks.
Hell, at her age I had three kids to feed,
Not that I'd trade them for a hundred more degrees,

But she's been fancy-free her whole damned
Life. Admittedly — part of her appeal.
Could never figure how she slipped the net —
Mystery girl, Maggie of the books.

I was mateless, dateless, and she was damn
Near a vision, G-rated like a Disney flick:
"Gidget Graduates and Finds a Job,"
Or, better, "Pollyanna Falls in Love."

So there I was, crass Mel the hooky cop,
And there *she* is, falling for *me* for chrissake,
A gift-wrapped virgin I couldn't keep. I did
Play at losing myself to find myself.

Went cold-turkey on tobacco. Pictured
Kids climbing out of windows, the house so full of them;
Me a Mormon bishop, passing by the bars
My uncles keep open. Tried to learn to dance.

That really would have gotten my ex.
The final papers duly signed and me
Waltzing in monkey-suits in church cultural
Halls. But if I don't know by now

That marriage ain't no bare-assed fairy tale —. Drank
Two solid months the summer I broke it off.
Then Cindy came along. No Mormon Church
To keep *us* from shacking up — *or* getting hitched.

I'm not saying you can outclass a Rolls Royce —
But can you really see me driving one?
OK. I wanted to. Tell you something else. If Maggie
Just snapped her fingers I'd be in her bed.

Amazing how she took my best yawning
Behavior for a sign I thought
The whole thing had a future. Chasms
Between us sometimes. That's what you call them. Chasms.

Like the time she asked me how an orgasm
Felt. Can you *imagine* her not knowing? Chasms.
And still she thought that we could make it. Try
Reasoning with rose-colored glasses. Try.

If she'd been born in the church . . . maybe then.
But a convert? Geez. How could I win? My ex denouncing
Christianity as patriarchal rot —
Maggie running to her bishop for advice.

Her consciousness so far from being raised
She'd yet to see herself as a grown woman.
Interviews to check her worthiness?
They couldn't see it? And me share her with that?

Sweet Maggie, treasure of Sierra Madre.
Loved her? Stripped down to her pagan self . . .
Hell. I would only disappoint her.
But she never thought so. Never. Can you beat that?

The Viewing

Point of yet another unmarked road, space
To stretch and finish off our food, as still
As the sloping fields above the cliffs and hushed
As the flat ruff nudging the idle quay.
We walked out to the far end of the pier,
Our biscuits salted by the slightest wind.

Perceptions wrecked, strange instincts woke
As we observed the water's shallow set.
Before gray water focused into slate,
The image slowly registered as shark.
Leviathan long as the pier was wide,
Tethered tail and snout inverted, strung like bait,

So undefiled, so clean, so sound
As might prohibit spoilage and deny
Our dying. I gauged the flaccid tail-fin
With the rope and looked to sea — a picnicker
Pinioned in a far Atlantic cove,
Surprised to doubt the languor of my island.

P. KAREN TODD

Imprints

Eucalyptus and date palms grow in my mind.
The smell of the sea from my nursery
Followed me eight years to Alabama
Like the gulls that followed my lunch to school.
It mingled with magnolia; it mocked the red clay.
And now the Rockies haunt me, like the negative
You see after staring at one color.

My parakeet is bonded to me,
But talks endlessly to his mirror.
How does he know his own?
Like his neon-colored feathers
And the hollow in his bone,
It grows.

After you left, I could still see you
There, where you lay beside me,
Imprinted on your pillow,
A shadow behind my eyes.

In the Ossuary

Chipping off bits of matrix rock
from millennia-old ribs, I wonder:
Where in the just-formed Genetic void
did God find bone-dust enough to mold
a Triceratops skull big as a car?
Did he chuckle when, one moment
in those Seven Days, he designed
Archaeopteryx, whose feathered wings,
they say, were made to catch flies
        and not to fly?

And how do Creation Scientists
battle with skeletons rising from earth
like Jason's army sprung from dragon's teeth?
Was God merely toying with his new ball of clay?
Or did he, with a wink of his all-seeing eye,
bury these riddles in the sure and certain hope
   of excavation?

Christmas Present

I could picture you: Quixote in a bathrobe,
Tilting at raindrops. And when Santanas blew,
You tossed in your bed like the eggs on the branch.
Mother, how did hummingbirds manage without you?

The nest is the size of half a hen's egg,
Mortared with spider webs and bits of bright green.
   I am five; you are showing me
   How to mix salt clay to make a gift.
Mandarin oranges cluster like grapes,
Plump with sun, late in December.
   I am nine; we are picking wild plums in humid August
   In Tennessee — tart jam for Christmas cookies.
The mother bird is a flashing green dart. She pumps nectar
Into her brood and scolds away finches twice her size.
   I am twelve; we eat kolače
   And sing carols beside a pine fire.
We watch their growth daily, from the kitchen and closer.
They are ugly, really — two beetles in a basket.
   Sixteen; we laugh at home movies.
   (Do they make baby buggies anymore?)

One of the fledglings fell from the nest.
Those are the odds in nature, I tell you.
But the morning it hailed, I went out in my robe
And held your umbrella over them, too.

Open Range, Wyoming

On Wyoming's genderless open range
There are no tall mountains, no hills with sage
Down, no cupped shadows, no blushes, flowers—
What bushes there are splay thin-leaved
And creep close to the sand on gnarled knuckles.
There are no pine shadows, no stippling lakes,
No pools, puddles—only deep swimming eyes
Of upright animals: sun-bleaching pronghorn
With obsidian tines; stray cattle set low
To earth, stumped by sun and short showers.
Clouds of horses blow across the highway,
Hides tinted from the golden, unsettling dust.
A gray spotted one, ears back,
Cleaves from the rear and moves like a wedge
Into the small middle of the herd.

          How all of these
Keep from eating each other in this endless place
Of meagerness, I cannot fathom, where no streams
Alter the color, and sky, broader than any meadow,
An unthinkable sea, parallels indefinite land;
Where antelope stand or sway, and seem to be
The only vegetation for seasons.

The Servant Girl

Never seek to tell thy love
Love that never told can be;
For the gentle wind does move
Silently, invisibly
— BLAKE

The servant girl is moving by the table.
Daily she brings us apples, rosy red,
And hickory nuts in their wrinkled, tawny shells.
Nursing the yellow poppies she has quickly cut
And brought under the houselight, she vases them.
A wisteria spray she's tucked inside her collar
Compares its lavender against her skin
And nods in her movement; a gust of sassafras,
An unseen spectre here, hovers in the room.
Perhaps it is on her hands. From her basket,
A cup of some dark berries, shining like coal;
Thin, moist ferns, some peaches, and a strange
Wild lily she has no doubt found by the river.
She seems to see the windowglass and hour of day
By the appearance of the sun on its gold hooves.
It walks unthought of by her in the room.
She sees our paintings changing after noon—

Landscapes, like windows on the wall
That move in the yellow, turning curves of the day.
This morning, while the grass was cool and yet
A lake in watery waves, she passed and saw
The baneberry upright in its spiny-red veins,
Looking at her from all sides, its long-stalked
Eyes pressing into the air, and no moss grew
Around it. She broke it off and brought it here.
It sits like a god on the high china shelf.
She is not without her faults: her first day here
She broke the looking-glass over the divan,
And she thinks to say I love you to someone loved
Is straining clarity, so she seldom prays
Except as an afterthought, the very same way
She'll step into the air on the edge of spring
And shed her petticoats and sweaters on the steps.
Each morning she opens the windows, pins the drapes,
And dries the last few slurs of night
Around the house. It is not her house.
Then it's through the door and out into the mist,
Making a dark trail through the argent grasses,
Barefoot, damp, and pliant like a sapling —
A touch of Daphne. When she comes into the room
We lapse into silence, but she doesn't hear.
She is like an aphid on a winding leaf
Staring through water beads with unwondering eyes.

Horseshoe Canyon: the Wall Paintings

Suns, sands, and winds render everything ghost.
Wall paintings in the canyon say:
We have no will. Canyon walls,
Flowers as thin as our children are will.

No love, only the worship of flesh:
Flesh of water, skins of light,
Brawn, cornmeats, bones and breasts,
Singing, ever before our eyes.
No hate, though there is the vengeance of loss.
Our knives are the teeth of this place; death
Goads us into the rock
And out of the rock.

We are as in the water we drink.
We sleep as in the flowers that change.
Sun brings together hunger and meat.
Moon divides the living stars.

Our gods stand by in the yellow cliffs.
Our prayers do not ask; we call to us
The pleasure deer, the body rain.
Our fathers do not abandon us.

We have visions, but not of ease,
With the writhing tree, the mud-sleeping toad,
The dry raven in the rock.
We see sand and devils of thirst.
We know the slow swiftness of blood.

There is no waking; we are veiled in the sun.
At night, we dream the moon and her flocks.

JOHN W. SCHOUTEN

Coming Home in the Evening

Lightning rings the valley
lighting empty haylofts, stealing
the light from the trees,
and after each flash I listen
for thunder.
It doesn't come, except
as an afterthought.
An uneasy breeze dusts
over the road, hisses
away through the grass and then . . .
the house, the light
behind the drapes, the car
dark in the drive.
You'll be on the couch,
feet curled beneath you,
a book in your lap or some
piece of handiwork . . .
A train on the outbound track,
there'll be others in the night.
You'll sleep through them
but I'll hear: horns fading,
boxcars rumbling away like dreams.

Rain Coming

The limbs of the sycamore flatten
out against this Utah sky
like the lines of a road map.
There's a breeze.
I can almost smell the distant
blackness, the rising Columbia.
At night sometimes it turns
on itself, flows backward
seeking its source,
and the black-mouthed Chinook
ride it home. I've seen it
from a car window sailing
down the gorge, waves and debris
rolling gently upstream,
silver backs lapping the surface,
going home.
That dark eastward flow.

Night Walk

It was nighttime in the back lot.
My father, on one knee beside me,
pointed to the sky,
a blackboard with chalk stars
and strange shapes. He taught me
to find the hunter and his dog,
the bear and her cub,
and seven sisters of shining glass.

Tonight I walk alone
through the quiet neighborhood.
Winter comes. The trees rattle.
By the streetlamp in front of my house
a shadow overtakes me.
It walks on ahead, growing taller.
I turn up the walk; the shadow
flows into the grass
and is lost like the stars at sunrise.

Early Morning in Mapleton

It's cool, cold
        for June. The chill
wakes us. I put a quilt on the bed,
we make love, you curl
into sleep.
        At the window I hear
soft conversations, trees waking.
Color bleeds into the valley,
you turn,
        breathe
deeply and resettle, the canyon
walls are two cupped hands
filling with milk.

Buttoning my coat I close
the door behind me, the canyon
breeze
        rolls off a slow
hill of rye. I cross the road, climb
the neighbor's gate and shake
hands with the tall
        grass
on the ditchbank, cows watch
with white faces.
At a rise in the pasture
        I turn
to see the house, white, still,
I think of you sleeping.
Dew flashes
        on the grass, the back
of my neck grows warm
and suddenly, I feel planted.

Divorce

With the heat at the end of August,
I am glad I sleep alone
And roll over on your side of the bed
Where the sheets are still cool.
I recall a December as I lay
Delicate and shivering,
Awake and naked on my wedding night.

In Celebration of a Daughter

More your father's child
Than ever any mother's thing—
Given in love, for love, by love,
We assume his name, become
More him than he is.
For though he only is he,
We, reproduced of his love,
Grow beyond him,
Beyond what he has given.
You, enchanting child, you
Forced your way between my hips,
Found your way onto my breast,
And when, tiny mythical thing,
You embraced my heart—
All that was not you
Found itself already shrinking.

From the Next Weird Sister

It matters not that my ankles are shapely and graceful,
Or that once, and I remember it well,
They said I had a splendid head of hair —
Perhaps the loveliest in all of Scotland.

One need not be a beldam to be a witch.
It takes only a desperate malignant need
To which there can be no relinquishment.
Be saucy and over-bold.
Your charms enough will change you.

For now the sun is setting,
And our clan meets again.
Here on the heath we spread the spoils of our battle,
And offer them to vacant, sable skies.
The fair men have called foul fair
And the foul men have called fair foul.
The fog is lifting,
But the filth in the air still remains.

Sometimes I wish I were a birth-strangled babe.
Then at least my finger would have a price.
And I might be understood
Or might understand the unknown powers.
But I was destined to live,
And am driven to accomplish deeds without names.

Come away, come away, come away.
When labor is too great —
Then is when a birth occurs.
I, mother of maggots,
I lay the eggs of my brain in night visions;
There to incubate, molt and corrode,
There to pardon and poison all entrails.

And what of you?
It matters not that your neck is slender —
Or you, that your breasts are warm and supple.
You, with that raging void —
You too can be a midnight hag.
It occurs to us all, at one time or another,
When a broken heart is the gift and the wound,
Sin can be a soothing salve.

The charm is wound up.
Sisters, let us take leave.
Something wicked this way comes —
We go in search of newts and a messiah.

The Next Weird Sister Attempts Repentance

Thinking it had been a while
since she had felt god's grace
(one should feel sorry,
loving one's own end) —
she thought she felt sorry,
bowed her head, opened locks
for the air, made a hell-broth
(can done be undone?).
She thought she felt sorry,
for the seeds of all
things yet uncreated
(he knows thy thoughts),
for a child with a tree in his hands
(who can impress the forest?),
for where she had never been
about, about — wayward
(show the grief his heart).
Thinking heaven is murky —
she thought she felt god's grace:
give me . . . give me . . .
then thought of killing swine.

The Next Weird Sister Bathes in the River Jordan

You have seen her in the water, at dawn—
For the Jordan is not deep.
She moves, a thing amphibian,
As easy in water as in air.
She steps into the depth of water
With arms extended, arms empty,
Asking for all things,
Miscarried of Eve, insider to loneliness.
And if you have not seen her,
You have seen Miriam and all the women following
With timbrels and with dances,
Like circles on water, entering and reentering.

Water is a circle moving through circles:
The medium of memories.
In water there is no removal.
All which evaporates will condense.
(For who can say when the last tide will
Pull from the angle of the earth?)
You have seen her in the water,
Or if not her, your neighbor's daughter
Playing in the brackish street curbs,
With no certain dwelling place.

She steps from the water
As if she were conceived of chaos,
Thinking her arms still empty.
But you, who have been happy and good
(Have you not many mothers?),
You know all things were given her,
Even at her conception.
She proceeds, without knowing
The possibility of satisfaction,
But you have seen, and you know . . .
For her hands have touched the water.

LANCE LARSEN

Light

A boy comes selling light,
no badges or letters of introduction,
just a paper sack of no-name bulbs
and a story about wanting to visit
his grandfather in Escondido. All this
on a morning so yellow that apricot buds,
tight as fists, threaten to unsmile.
But I believe him — for two dollars
I get variable wattage and a sweepstake
chance at a telescope. And safety.
I wrap my bulb in cashmere and lock it away.
For now I'll use G. E. bulbs.
But later, on a night when the moon
wears its blood in a smile
and the angels of light have been coffined
and the earth reels through the air
on the back of a drunken mule,
I'll replace the bulb on the porch.
Then from my front room, I'll watch,
like any patient child of the covenant,
for the destroying angel to pass me by.

After Fishing

The headlights
catch the shine
of wet quills
and pooled eyes.
You kill the engine
and we stalk
through twin wedges
of yellow light.

I stare at the backs
of your knees
where your pants
bunch and loosen
like widening jaws.
I take two steps
for each of yours.
My sneakers drown
in your prints.

I shiver
at the bundle
of smashed flesh
spilling innards
like wet worms.
"It's been hit," you say
hefting a stone
yellow and round
as a pumpkin
and mincing backwards
to straddle the porcupine
with black boot toes.

When you lift your hands I turn away.
The blow stills the head
but the nerved legs
brush at air like the wings
of a shot sparrow
dropping to earth
on a broken breeze.

Later, bundled in wool,
I watch you tread
embers into dust
under a pine-laced moon.
I close my eyes to the stars,
the lake, the sifting grey
that melts your shadow into trees.
When I feel your hand, smoky warm,
I curl against your palm
and give myself to sleep.

Dreaming Among Hydrangeas

My mother's been sleeping on the patio.
The heat, she says. She has an army cot
and a stack of paperbacks. After the news,
she sits among hydrangeas, flipping pages,
tented in yellow light from the lamp
I dragged from the garage.
Sometimes she writes my father.
I have a picture of him with a string of camels.

Saturday nights she plays pinochle
with the Zabriskies. She cuts up cantaloupe
and comes home with an empty bowl.
Tonight she'll dream of a white moon
and figs red as open mouths, of palms shading
a pool where a bearded man swims naked,
and fish, like darting fingers,
move cleanly against the stars.

Tadpoles

Asleep beside me, my wife dreams of babies,
three or four swimming slow circles like tadpoles.
She feels them inside her, slippery warm.
I watch the walls and think of a girl I hugged
at sock-hops, pigeon chested, safe as a brother.
Her name was Lori. We were twelve.

That fall the girls watched a film. We knew.
Amy Jarvis started first—bleeding like she'd
cut off a finger. Martha told us at recess.
"Amy,"—it was a conjured name, her eyes
strange as stars. Her body was the weather.
We were sailors, watchful and afraid.

Lori cried because she was slower. I held her hand.
In the band room. On the mats. She smelled
of rain. Hugging her was like hugging myself,
like touching a flower you hope will never open.
I touched older girls and felt myself dying,
felt the quiet annihilation of losing pieces.

With my wife it is the same. I wake her
with kisses, pin her against shadows.
She touches me. This is how she explains
her dreams, how she refuses to explain.
They hang like whispers in a foreign movie,
the same phrase over and over, pleasurable tiny stabs.

Passing the Sacrament
at Eastgate Nursing Home

Every third Sunday we gave them
bread of another world.
Usually it was George and me.
We'd pull up in my dad's Monte Carlo,
brisk as bishops, solemn as high councilors.
We filled cups in the janitor's closet,
looking only once at the wrinkled
Miss July behind the door.

When it came time, we broke and passed
sliding between wheel chairs and walkers
with the grace of nurses, never smiling,
decorous in our sneakers and clip-on ties.
Of course, we had our moments.
There was the guy who stood on his chair
and yelled for a Bingo card, and the lady
who started hugging my leg and calling me Jesus.
But we kept composure — talked them back
into the quiet of their lunacy,
unknotted their fingers from our arms.

We always took the slow road home.
If it was summer, we drove by the pool,
scouting the matched perfection,
the bikini splendor, of the Hunsaker twins.
And when we had money, we headed for Winchell's.
Sometimes on the last mile home,
with the windows down and the sun
buttering the road, I'd think of Eastgate,
how I carried trays to bed-ridden members —
the lady in 243 who wore her breasts at her waist.
Craning forward, she opened her mouth,
and I with clean and careful hands
laid the bread on her tongue.

A Philanthropist Speaks to His Lawyer

I don't mind giving it away — the estate,
the refineries, the beach front in Bermuda,
my Shakespeare folios and Rothko rectangles.
Stipulate that no one touch my organs.
When my heart gives, pack me in dry ice
and send me south — Lima or Santiago.
Hire a driver, pay him twice what he asks.
Drive until you find a hobbling woman
with veined calves. If she turns down a dirt road
where squealing pigs jump from her path,
if the smoke behind the hills hangs stiffly
like drying wash, if her house puts on
a scrubbed face when she opens the gate,
then tell her I'm a cousin who needs to be buried.
Notice the sadness in her braids,
the evenings pressed into her heavy skirt.
After rubbing me with scented oils,
she will lay me, smiling, my hands crossed,
between her sofa and a broken radio.
Women will kiss the glass over my face.
Children will feel my blood pooling in the rain.
If the neighbors ask to build a shrine,
point them to a mangled light post,
tell them I died violently. Materials?
Whatever they can find or steal.
Small as a doll house. Filled with crucifix,
Virgin, plastic San Martin, and tapers,
flickery as underwater beams. Forget the vault.
Put me into a hole with the indigents.
A grave digger will walk my skull through air.
Let me try my new legs on my own schedule.
A windless morning it will be, blue,
a little sullen, the fig trees voiceless
in their heavy leaves. Birds are slower then,
toads hide in the ferns. I'm tired.
I feel it most in the afternoons.

PHILIP WHITE

Seed

I was born in the desert
Brigham made bloom.
I was reared among the dry grass.
Measured water
came each two weeks,
and even God
could not make it reach
to the far fence corners.
The dirt there was white,
hard as chalk. Every few feet
were the niggard weedflowers,
blooms so tight
you had to stoop
to see their hard yellowing.

His cottonwoods
are now a hundred feet high,
trunks five feet thick,
bark greyer and deader
than barn shakes.
I am an old man pouring water
into dirt cracks, praying
against the disadvantage
of seed.

The Citypeople Speak

Up on the hill, a rough
half–mile outside of town.
Anyone could see.
It was around noon

when they finally
lugged him up.
Men around him drew
back among us, faces

shrunken like clay.
A few stones braced
the upright. Anyone
could see the woman

bent up there. From here,
her song was like a cry.

DANIELLE BEAZER

An Awakening

Emma fans herself by the sea
and watches her children
gather sand on their bodies
while Leon stands near her,
a dark keystone
between herself and her desire.

She is like the young filly
who whisked grain from our palms
but trembled her mane and shied from our hands
when we reached to touch her neck.
She is like the woman you photographed
sitting on the fence
her feet against the chipped slats,
balancing her arms out
like a pyramid.

The filly rolled and dusted her auburn coat
behind me,
and you said, "Don't fall,"
as I leaned forward
and caught myself.

Over the Other Side of the Country

I

Walking home
he recalls a lover
from college days.
The leaves, curled and wet,
remind him.
It has been years;
no name comes to mind.
A cat bats her tail.
He lets her indoors
then sits by the window
studying the curtains.
The cat jumps to his lap
her paws on his chest.
Stroking her spine,
"Tahti—to what do I owe this pleasure?"

II

What were his best years?
He thinks,
and cannot put them all in one.
A time when he was ten
watching his father
tie wires for the fencing
tying them so tightly
a red flush would rise along the palms
and suddenly he misses his father.

The birth of his son
the tiny feet fanned like angel's wings
(then Melinda leaving
taking the boy)

A girl in a bar, not over 25,
asked him between puffs on a Lucky,
"So, like, what's it like at 40?"
"The same as 20, only paunchier."
Of course she laughed and as they danced
    she whispered to his earlobe
how she could take off ten years.

III   *Melinda*

He remembers waking to a movement from her
    and watching her pad to the window
        before morning really came.
        She breathed on the glass
        and formed a round kiss
        that would dirty the pane
        when the mist disappeared.
        She stood there for minutes
    goose bumps rising along her legs.
He imagined her breasts firming to the cold
    but she stood there for minutes
        and never really came back.

IV

    Outside the rain crackles —
    red from the brake lights of passing cars
red from the ABC store's neon sign down the street
    red from the wet brick doorstep
    incubating under the porch light.

    And so they were gone.
    He had lost them somewhere
    behind the fences, the window
        the angel's wings.
    Cold mornings and warm ones
        wet nights like this
        a cat, a curtain
        a nameless lover
        living somewhere
over the other side of the country.

The Next Day

Of all the days, his was the quietest.
No morning ever rose with such slow colors —
The saffron hues fanning open the sky
Lengthening over the Blue Ridge
With before-dawn sleepiness,
Resting on frosted barbed wire
Pale splintered posts
The diadems in the dying grass,
Filling frozen hoof prints made by
Cows nudging and rubbing to crop
The blades over the fence before
The air turned winter grey,
Before the ground like poured plaster
Stiffened.
Through the doorway I watched this day come,
Remembering all the night before
When I pressed my forehead against the glass
Trying to find a face somewhere
In the moon.

TIMOTHY LIU

Martial Art

I've hung up the white robe
for good. I'm broke.
My books have crashed
to the floor. I'm not
anywhere near home.
I believe my eyes
have committed more crime
than the blind man
waiting on death row.

No one believes in death
by fire anymore
though the coastlines burn
with toxic waste,
St. John's vision
on the six o'clock news.
If I close my door
on Patmos, will anyone
hold it against me
if I refuse to wash
my hands in the river?

I want the world
dining at my table,
feeding off scraps
they've never considered.
Before they can finish
putting out the flame
of their seafood shishkebabs
I'll break their boards
like a blackbelt
against the grain,
and let each splinter smoulder
in the eye of God.

Variations on Death

1

After all, summer was over
and the heat had begun
to nest in your mother's attic.
We sat on the veranda,
watching hornets dive from the roof
into the bougainvillea
blooming above our heads.
For hours I tore the petals open.
With fuchsia in your hair,
you sang fragments of a melody
I've forgotten. But I remember
the black notes I plucked
from your lips, tight
as the strings on that Chinese lute
my father played at dawn.
In the house, mother spun silk
from cocoons she had raised
in darkness. She never heard
sadder songs. We danced
as they danced: like paper
lanterns in the wind.

2

You fed me dinner and cocked
the hammer in my head. We left
your wedding china in the sink,
under a cloud of suds. Did you think
that my chambers were loaded
or did you notice my eyes
were cleaned out like the fish
you broiled in the oven?
You picked the bones clean.
This morning I found a scale
on my pillow case, shining
like beached glass, and knew
that the tide must have come
and gone while I slept, washing
our carved names out to sea.

3

The girl is lying with her face
toward the ground, reading about life
after death. She does not see
what the dead have seen on their backs
after the final nail was driven
through wood. The autumn shade falls
like a leaf onto her open book.
Below her, coffins burst open like seeds.
After turning another page of light,
she rolls herself over, asleep
in a field of white crosses.

Paper Flowers

Your mother made perfect
lotus blossoms from tissue paper
until the Red Guard forced her
to kneel on the washboard;
your Sunday dress shivered
in the room where you hid
under the floor. The tears that year
were enough for a life-time
of loads down by the Shanghai
as they cracked her porcelain skin
with purple welts, each hour
growing darker. The God of silence
carried your cries as you buried
your face in the flowers of spring
drenched with storm. Your father
would have folded you in his arms
had he survived the clubbing
at the Bible study — no one did.
Years later you burned your dress,
a memorial for your mother
in prison. Still you'll scream
some nights, clutching the pocket
New Testament against your breast,
each page a faded yellow petal.

Cathedral

My steps are worn echoes
under the arches bending
their weight to the cross
hung darkly by stained glass
where I knew I'd find you.
I sit in the last pew, unnoticed
by your voice, rehearsing
before God the song of our sins,
accompanied by your hands,
the ivory trembling, your lips
a bitter cup spilling onto stone.
Soon the walls enclose us
like the mind of Christ,
each falling note a thorn
in the crown of blood.

Death Calls

I made you some breakfast.
What else could I do after
waking you from dreams.
The moth which flittered by
last night lies motionless
on the sill. No alarm rang,
only the phone. Now breath
spreads across frosted glass
where you watch October's
first snow dust the lawn.
You didn't hear the toaster
kick or the bacon shrinking
in the iron pan. You didn't
notice that the cold edges
were charred, that I passed
the salt you always took.

Final Preparations

Porro Unum Est Necessarium
— MATTHEW ARNOLD

I am the only one at church
    with my *Norton Anthology*
preparing for tomorrow's final.
        The pulpit will be vacant,
and still light will break
        through stained glass, bright
as wings of a gull, circling
        deserted beaches in search
of trash. The fallen words
        from His lips could never be
contained in all the sheets
        that yellow and crack with age.
But enough has been saved.
        And if God chooses to speak
from the leaves I've gathered
        and spread before the altar,
will He refuse my offering:
        my life of letters? I cannot
retract a word, only repent
        of glitches I have made.
When He comes, the statues
        will crumble, whole cities
tremble, paper burn away.
        With rubble we'll be judged
by books, by all the mouths
        who've suffered since
the world began, our voices
        unveiling His face of darkness.
Who can abide the glory of One
        who freezes shadow onto stone,
tears the charred sentences out
        of our throats, the singing ashes
of ink and paper our final prayer?
        How jealous a god He is.
I speak while I have breath,
        before the sand I stand upon
melts to glass, and the whole earth
        is shot like a marble.

*Hymns
and
Songs*

PAUL L. ANDERSON

We Meet Again As Sisters

We meet again as sisters
On this the Sabbath day
To worship God together,
To testify and pray.
Now may the Holy Spirit,
Descending like a dove,
Enlarge our minds with knowledge
And fill our hearts with love.

We meet to plan our service
To neighbors now in need.
May charity and kindness
Inspire our ev'ry deed.
And as we use our talents
For good and noble ends,
May God be our companion
And angels be our friends.

We meet to sing together
The praises of our Lord,
To seek our exaltation
According to his word.
To ev'ry gospel blessing
The Lord has turned the key,
That we, with heav'nly parents,
May sing eternally.

KATHRYN R. ASHWORTH

A Weathered Cross Beside the Wall

A weathered cross beside the wall
    Supports the climbing rose,
And sun within the garden warms it
    In the winter snows.

Red thorns will guard its budding
    When springtime comes again
As roses bloom upon the limbs
    To hide the cross from men.

They had thee, Lord, assume the cross,
    But hoped to thrust thee down;
The thorns did not defend thee,
    But barbed thy braided crown.

For thee the quiet garden gleamed
    An empty place of pain
Where thorns turned inward at thy pores
    Drawing crimson rain.

For thee whose beauty is a rose
    To bear the fate of thorns
Required a love as deep as grief
    When God thy Father mourns.

What fears, then, thorns upon my heart,
    Would keep thy hand away,
Thy hand that blossoms like a rose
    Upon a winter day?

MARILYN MCMEEN BROWN

Thy Servants Are Prepared

Thy servants are prepared
To teach thy word abroad,
To gather in thy sheep
To thee, O Lamb of God.

Let these, thy servants, speak
With heart and voice of youth,
And fill their world's dark lamps
With light, the flame of truth.

In all of Zion's stakes
Thy love shall conquer night,
While darkness draws away
From thy revealing light.

KAREN LYNN DAVIDSON

Each Life That Touches Ours for Good

Each life that touches ours for good
Reflects thine own great mercy, Lord;
Thou sendest blessings from above
Thru words and deeds of those who love.

What greater gift dost thou bestow,
What greater goodness can we know
Than Christ-like friends, whose gentle ways
Strengthen our faith, enrich our days.

When such a friend from us departs,
We hold forever in our hearts
A sweet and hallowed memory,
Bringing us nearer, Lord, to thee.

For worthy friends whose lives proclaim
Devotion to the Savior's name,
Who bless our days with peace and love,
We praise thy goodness, Lord above.

EDWARD L. HART

Our Savior's Love

Our Savior's love
Shines like the sun with perfect light,
As from above
It breaks thru clouds of strife.
Lighting our way,
It leads us back into his sight,
Where we may stay
To share eternal life.

The Spirit, voice
Of goodness, whispers to our hearts
A better choice
Than evil's anguished cries.
Loud may the sound
Of hope ring till all doubt departs,
And we are bound
To him by loving ties.

Our Father, God
Of all creation, hear us pray
In rev'rence, awed
By thy Son's sacrifice.
Praises we sing.
We love thy law; we will obey.
Our heav'nly King,
In thee our hearts rejoice.

The Gentle Way

(for David O. McKay)

He left to other men the path
    To wealth, that turns to clay;
He left to others hate and wrath,
    And sought the gentle way.

Though life was filled with joy and pain
    And threatening decay,
He never challenged God's design,
    But chose the gentle way.

Temptations offered subtle cures
    For ills, and time to pay;
He stripped the mask off ugly lures,
    And kept the gentle way.

He earned the sweetest word known—peace,
    Striving day by day
To live to the last breath's release
    In love, the gentle way.

DONNELL HUNTER

How Glorious is the Voice We Hear

To President Harold B. Lee

How glorious is the voice we hear from heaven!
Now prophets drive the darkness from our lives.
Hearken to their counsel; honor their priesthood;
Receive the word our loving Father gives.

Our prophet speaks to show the way to Zion,
A refuge for the saints whose hearts are pure.
Follow his example; treasure his message;
Sustain his call and love will cast out fear.

His voice now calls to every tongue and nation.
Each ear shall hear and every eye shall see.
Listen to the Gospel; keep the commandments;
Forsake the world; his truths will make you free.

Our Father lead and bless the living prophet.
Protect him where he travels through this world.
Help him while he teaches light in life's darkness
And guides us back to thy eternal fold.

BRUCE W. JORGENSEN

For Bread and Breath of Life

*"Always bearing about in the body the dying of
the Lord Jesus, that the life also of Jesus might
be made manifest in our body."*

— 2 COR. 4:10

Our God who flamed within a tree
And spoke the law to shape our way,
We consecrate this hour to thee
And ask thy hearing as we pray.

Our Brother nailed upon a tree,
We eat and drink, and view thy death,
And live thy law in love, that we
May all be quickened by thy breath.

The Light Come Down

Just a dusty country boy
Praying in the trees,
Knocked out flat and speechless,
Again up on his knees
And the light come down,
Lord, the light come down.

Sharper than suns he sweated in,
It slapped that April mud,
It withered the one that threatened him
And stunned him where he stood.
    Yes, the light come down,
    Lord, it did come down.

And he was just fourteen,
Mixed up, and read your book
And took you at your word
and asked — and Lord,
    You let the light come down,
    O Lord, a comin down.

Old Adam had a farmer's son
And Abraham did too —
All made of mud but you made em good
And brought em home to you,
    For the light come down,
    It always did come down.

So Lord look down on country boys
That stink and puzzle and pray,
And strike the light to blind their sight
And make their night your day.
    O let the light come down,
    Yes, bring the light on down.

And bless you, Lord, for country boys,
Each hungry mother's son
Treading the furrow his father plowed
Just like your single son
    When you and him come down,
    When you the light come down.

CLARA W. MCMASTER

Teach Me to Walk in the Light

Teach me to walk in the light of his love;
Teach me to pray to my Father above;
Teach me to know of the things that are right;
Teach me, teach me to walk in the light.

Come, little child, and together we'll learn
Of his commandments, that we may return
Home to his presence, to live in his sight—
Always, always to walk in the light.

Father in Heaven, we thank thee this day
For loving guidance to show us the way.
Grateful, we praise thee with songs of delight!
Gladly, gladly we'll walk in the light.

REID N. NIBLEY

I Know My Father Lives

I know my Father lives and loves me too.
The Spirit whispers this to me and tells me it is true,
And tells me it is true.

He sent me here to earth, by faith to live his plan.
The Spirit whispers this to me and tells me that I can,
And tells me that I can.

JOHN SEARS TANNER

Bless Our Fast, We Pray

On bended knees, with broken hearts,
We come before thee, Lord,
In secret and in open prayer —
Oh, wilt thou speak thy word?

Feed thou our souls, fill thou our hearts,
And bless our fast, we pray,
That we may feel thy presence here
And feast with thee today.

We've shared our bread with those in need,
Relieved the suff'ring poor.
The stranger we have welcomed in —
Wilt thou impart thy store?

Feed thou our souls, fill thou our hearts,
And bless our fast, we pray,
That we may feel thy presence here
And feast with thee today.

As witnesses, we gather here
To thank, and to attest
Of mercies and of miracles —
Oh, still our lives so bless!

Feed thou our souls, fill thou our hearts,
And bless our fast, we pray,
That we may feel thy presence here
And feast with thee today.

EMMA LOU THAYNE

Where Can I Turn for Peace?

Where can I turn for peace?
Where is my solace
When other sources cease to make me whole?
When with a wounded heart, anger, or malice,
I draw myself apart,
Searching my soul?

Where, when my aching grows,
Where, when I languish,
Where, in my need to know, where can I run?
Where is the quiet hand to calm my anguish?
Who, who can understand?
He, only One.

He answers privately,
Reaches my reaching
In my Gethsemane, Savior and Friend.
Gentle the peace he finds for my beseeching.
Constant he is and kind,
Love without end.

Friends
and
Relations

JOHN DAVIES

For the Welsh Mormons

Roads under snapped peaks have eased us
from towns so small their children
glanced up. Sidetracked history rusts cars.
The sun tracks us through conditioned air
so even from Emigration Canyon
focal points relate. Steepled, the faith
not ours that's brought us along trails
people with our names helped make, glints
at desert. Salt Lake City in a moonscape

is a landing place. Those faceless facing
walls: when a big wind shook them,
yes they said to voices calling Jump
that gave them first the Atlantic,
yes to cholera, to hand carts heaved
a thousand miles into space under weather's
gritted teeth. All slipped land theirs
not their own. And, like new faith they'd wrapped
their lives around, keeping the desert out,

received this land. Blown to another world
on prayers, first they had to make it,
the sky striped red then stars flying.
Proposed: we should build as a nation
along the Jordan River with Elizabeth Lewis
as Queen. Rejected. But though parched —
two climates merging, heat drains
moisture almost memory — a New Wales breathed.
Sun blinked at the Spanish Fork eisteddfod.

At the university they helped build, my wife
is one of few who can translate them.
Their great-grandchildren who know London
do not know each other. Flight paths over Salt Lake

converge, fade out, as sky measures gain and loss
and soon, strong as the flight that brought us,
what we left will give us cloud country again
pierced by what's beyond, that must keep
changing and not changing to stay intact.

Driving the Provo River

(for Leslie Norris)

Leaving the car, horn bellowing,
that rode rocks into the canyon
you climb with your wife, daughter,
breathing and in skidmarked snow wait
for your life to catch you up.
Now the road's going straight.
You've rebounded, floating on thin air.
Drivers stop, speak urgent smoke
but police know the accidenting season:
welcome back, lucky the river's low.

Home later, why should you stop talking?
Lights at the edge of expectation
coming on like fires burn dinner plates
white, print swerves as a newspaper shakes your hand.
On the sports channel: bodybuilders.
Your eyes head south from bunched shoulders
through gulleys of the bicep, outcrops
of weathered leg. When you turn in bed,
strange how your stomach arrives late.
Time for self-discipline, you swear,
self-everything, then fail to sleep.

Next day remembered musclemen like pet shops
wriggle and twitch. Wife, daughter, friends
at the ends of letters, offer selfscapes
in proportion. Thing level off. But as if to prove
heights gained are only canyons upside down,
now the lights come on like lights.

What Doesn't End When the Year Ends

It's over, the goodwill season, and even
our tree still switched on in hopes of a second
coming looks snuffed in the light of day.
Decorations hang around asking too much. Why not
just write cheques, suggest my poems.

Dwindling out of the distance, Jeff calls
with that smile on a tight leash. Is it
his job at the bank, some shadow he was born in?
Robust, eating as she drives, maybe Beth's
convinced him life isn't his natural element.

The river's snow dome swirls.
Trees like ropes strong from branches,
hovering, stripe both banks plumping for low profiles
that panes of ice slide past unbroken.
Against the current, magpies hang-glide.

Persuading stones to inch further,
though the river tows ice, even in branched
shadow not one stone seems to move.
And yet, the art all art thirsts to mirror,
in Utah Lake mountains see themselves.

At the bridge when I look back, driftings
away from me switch to running downriver my way.
Now trees give way to hills. Eyes
skim straight where reeds and flatness
sigh over long perspectives, a heron

staring fish into its radius pinions the lake,
and though even this new season creaks,
a shining skates me on as if everything's
been crushed into one small part of the country
white and only once this once.

BREWSTER GHISELIN

Rattlesnake

I found him sleepy in the heat
And dust of a gopher burrow,
Coiled in loose folds upon silence
In a pit of the noonday hillside.
I saw the wedged bulge
Of the head hard as a fist.
I remembered his delicate ways:
The mouth a cat's mouth yawning.
I crushed him deep in dust,
And heard the loud seethe of life
In the dead beads of the tail
Fade, as wind fades
From the wild grain of the hill.

Fragment of a Dialogue

For Gene England

Firm on our atoll, desert
Heart of bitter mirage,
Doubting believer, I stand with you
Sipping this brackish communion,
Breaking hard bread of alternatives —
Either a waste ocean
Or an infinite ocean of hope:
Whether these shimmering fronds
Above us, mere palms, are illusion,
Or else or also those petals,
That one Dove hovering descending
Out of the garden of the sun
To brood the hopes of humanity —
Both of such beautiful credentials,
Blazoned on measureless dark.

In terrible splendor of dilemma,
Saints walk into the night
To be washed of fire.
                    They return to us
Saying, "This shade is cool
Under the wings and the boughs.
Let us not forget one another."

A View of Little Scope

Dinosaur National Monument

On the desolate hills by the river
(green like its name in the shallowing summer
after the bulging thrust of muddying runoff
in spring) in the fields of dust that yield
to the steep untillable ragged
and more ragged
wedges and gullies that gather
to the crests of stone,
the little lizards, whiplash
terror of flies and beetles
and shifty mist of midges in the shimmering summer
we share,
pause on a bulge of bonewhite stonegray rock
or run endlong on the shaft of it down to the crumble
that hides the rest
of the remnant of terror
that fed here once,
or they whip away in a flick
and are lost to us under the lacy light
of sage leaf and litter of stem
till the terror has passed,
that rules here now,
and will rule awhile;
and the water away by the sparse
willows and the fewer cottonwoods under
a vast of no clouds
lies like a font,
unstilled
and still,
the river,
glittering and paling to its far
fadings,
gliding and shining in its winding
on the waste,
on the pathway of the lost,
gleaming in enormous light.

Christmas in Utah

In barns turned from the wind
the quarter-horses
twitch their laundered blankets.
Three Steller's Jays,
crests sharp as ice,
bejewel the pine tree.
Rough cold out of Idaho
bundles irrational tumbleweed
the length of Main Street.

Higher than snowpeaks,
shriller than the frost,
a brazen angel blows his silent trumpet.

The Dark Months

Frost nails to the soil
the slots of deer.
Snow will cover them
the dark months of the year.

Waxwings strip from the branch
last fleshes of berry —
haw and firethorn nourish
their starving journey.

It is an eternal star
above the high Uintas
offers its untouched light,
its cold promises.

A Sea in the Desert

1.
A little sea
    in the night
      ran its inch of tide
    about the bole of the peach tree,
hesitated,
      came fawning to my door,
        cringed,
          fell away.

Its small crests,
    its ebb,
        broke my sleep.

2.
A little sea
    was running in the desert.
   It came in
      under the edges of the breeze,
a true sea,
      sharpening the air with salt,
        filling hourly through the night.

It remembered white ships
    clippers out of China
      freighted with tea and roses,
        sea-swans
    holding gales in their wings,
storms off the coast of fragrant Spain, snarling.

    It hurled
  against my walls
    its gathering whips and drums,
      dropped away,
its throat rattling with pebbles.

3.
I got up,
    opened my door
        to this unbelievable sea.

My yard was lit by silent moonlight.
Parched grasshoppers chirrupped in the ditches.

4.
But still the sea broke
    on the beaches of my ears.

My skull was a shell
 holding the noisy tides
pouring unseen over the desert.

5.
A man is moon to his own sea —
he draws it after him,
like a dog it follows him
the days of his life.

All that night I heard the sea make
and ebb, a sea formed
of grains of remembered oceans,
fed by rains and rivers

of days I have finished with.
It carried old sticks in its mouth.
In the morning a tide's detritus,
twigs, small round stones, a can,

lay in uneven lines
on the charred grass.

6.
A hermit thrush sings for me
in dry arroyos its liquid note.
I have heard in the desert
unrecognized birds, charmers,

lift up their single whistles,
long, separated, distant,
purified by distance, among
the grassless dunes.

I have thought them calling me.
I have heard the voices
of an invisible sea
whispering with boys'

voices, heard in its dry waves
the pattering of boys' feet
through the built canyons
of the past. I have heard

such singing. The mocking-bird
has sung for me. Each day
the waters of that sea
are rising blindly to the full.

WILLIAM STAFFORD

Scripture

In the dark book where words crowded together,
a land with spirits waited, and they rose and walked
every night when the book opened by candlelight—

A sacred land where the words touched the trees
and their leaves turned into fire. We carried it wherever
we went, our hidden scene; and in the sigh of snow coming down,

In the city sometimes a people without any book
drove tunneling by in traffic, eyes measuring
chances ahead, the red light at the end of the block—

Then sprung over that city a dark word like judgment
arched, every face turned into a soul
wandering the shadow of the tabernacle world.

Witness

This is the hand I dipped in the Missouri
above Council Bluffs and found the springs.
All through the days of my life I escort
this hand. Where would the Missouri
meet a kinder friend?

On top of Fort Rock in the sun I spread
these fingers to hold the world in the wind;
along that cliff, in that old cave
where men used to live, I grubbed in the dirt
for those cool springs again.

Summits in the Rockies received this diplomat.
Brush that concealed the lost children yielded
them to this hand. Even on the last morning
when we all tremble and lose, I will reach
carefully, eagerly through that rain, at the end—

Toward whatever is there, with this loyal hand.

The Farm on the Great Plains

A telephone line goes cold;
birds tread it wherever it goes.
A farm back of a great plain
tugs an end of the line.

I call that farm every year,
ringing it, listening, still;
no one is home at the farm,
the line gives only a hum.

Some year I will ring the line
on a night at last the right one,
and with an eye tapered for braille
from the phone on the wall

I will see the tenant who waits—
the last one left at the place;
through the dark my braille eye
will lovingly touch his face.

"Hello, is Mother at home?"
No one is home today.
"But Father—he should be there."
No one—no one is here.

"But you—are you the one . . . ?"
Then the line will be gone
because both ends will be home:
no space, no birds, no farm.

My self will be the plain,
wise as winter is gray,
pure as cold posts go
pacing toward what I know.

MAY SWENSON

That the Soul May Wax Plump

"He who has reached the highest degree of
emptiness will be secure in repose."
— A TAOIST SAYING

My dumpy little mother on the undertaker's slab
had a mannequin's grace. From chin to foot
the sheet outlined her, thin and tall. Her face
uptilted, bloodless, smooth, had a long smile.
Her head rested on a block under her nape,
her neck was long, her hair waved, upswept. But later,
at "the viewing," sunk in the casket in pink tulle,
an expensive present that might spoil, dressed
in Eden's green apron, organdy bonnet on,
she shrank, grew short again, and yellow. Who
put the gold-rimmed glasses on her shut face, who
laid her left hand with the wedding ring on
her stomach that really didn't seem to be there
under the fake lace?

Mother's work before she died was self-purification,
a regimen of near starvation, to be worthy to go
to Our Father, Whom she confused (or, more aptly, fused)
with our father, in Heaven long since. She believed
in evacuation, an often and fierce purgation,
meant to teach the body to be hollow, that the soul
may wax plump. At the moment of her death, the wind
rushed out from all her pipes at once. Throat and rectum
sang together, a galvanic spasm, hiss of ecstasy.
Then, a flat collapse. Legs and arms flung wide,
like that female Spanish saint slung by the ankles
to a cross, her mouth stayed open in a dark O. So,
her vigorous soul whizzed free. On the undertaker's slab, she
lay youthful, cool, triumphant, with a long smile.

Above Bear Lake

Sky and lake the same blue,
and blue the languid mountain between them.
Cloud fluffs make the scene flow.
Greeny white poles of aspen snake up,
graven with welts and calluses where branches
dried and broke. Other scabs are lover-made:
initials dug within linked hearts and, higher,
some jackknifed peace signs.
A breeze, and the filtered light makes shine
a million bristling quills of spruce and fir
downslope, where slashes of sky and lake
hang blue — windows of intense stain. We take
the rim trail, crushing bloom of sage,
sniffing resinous wind, our boots in the wild,
small, everycolored Rocky Mountain flowers.
Suddenly, a steep drop-off: below we see the whole,
the whale of it — deep, enormous blue —
that widens, while the sky slants back to pale
behind a watercolored mountain.
Western Tanager — we call him "Fireface" —
darts ahead, we climb to our camp
as the sun slips lower. Clipped to the top
of the tallest fir, Olive-Sided Flycatcher,
over and over, fierce-whistles, "Whip!
Whip three bears! Whip, whip three bears!"

My Name was Called

I didn't know what would be done with me.
When my name was called. As when baptized
for the first time. A stiff black four-
cornered hat on. Afraid it would fall off.
My ears stuck out but couldn't grab to keep
it steady on my head slippery and small.
Wet and white the slick enamelled chair,
its pattern of holes in the metal seat
where the water drained. My spotted hand
went up to try to help to bring the velvet
investiture over my square-hatted head.
Awkward. Old bobble with straight short
hair, lashless eyes and smileless mouth.
My name was called. Heavy medallion on wide
blue ribbon hung swinging from my neck.
The Elder's white robe sloshed at his knees,
he held my wrists to my chest, backwards
pressed me under, dipped me blind in the
marble font under green-veined water.
My name was called. My eight-year-old head
didn't know what would be done.

Old teetering monkeylike babylike head
under black gold-tasselled stiff platter-
like hat, sixty years later, the naked ears
stick out. My name is called. Pulled up,
out of the deafening bubbles, boosted up
to sit in the white chair. Murmured over
my head the rapid redundant prayer. Wet
head bowed beneath the hands laid heavy there.
Warm, suggestively wet, my white ruffled
panties streamed in the slick seat.
The silk and velvet lifted. My spotted
hand went up. Awkward. Huge in merciless
light my face on screen in front of my
actual face. My little ignorant ugly patient
helpless head on screen, the freshest horror.
The greatest honor. Forced to confront,
but not forced to smile. Child eyes behind

old pouched lashless eyes, never again able
to soften the truth of my future face.
Face immersed, but still afloat over the years.
Head pressed under and blessed. Pulled up
and invested. I didn't know what would be
done, in the white dress or in the black,
when my name was called.

Editors' Commentary

New Tradition

EUGENE ENGLAND

Poetry is one of the arts of time as well as of language. Like music, it depends for its finest and fullest achievement on clear and subtle use of various kinds of rhythm—repetition and variation over time, of exact or similar stresses, silences, and phrases. Like prose, it is composed of words and therefore deals in concepts, ideas, and moral values as well as sounds; it has content as well as form. Language by nature uses sounds with less precision and variety than music, but a skilled poet, using the carefully developed resources for rhythmic expression in poetic forms, can control the remarkable effects of rhythm on emotion and cognition with more subtlety and power than the prose writer.

Mormon poets, probably because of their religious beliefs and experience, tend to emphasize content over form. Mormon poetry began in hymn texts, continued in competent narrative poetry about our martyred leaders and epic history, then settled into a heavily didactic mode in the 1880s that was named "Home Literature." (The name was given by its main advocate, Orson F. Whitney.) These traditions—hymns, narrative accounts of Mormon life, and "faith-promoting" verses—today continue strong and little-changed from the nineteenth century, published mainly in Latter-day Saint hymnbooks and the official magazines, the *Ensign*, the *New Era*, and the *Friend*, or exchanged among family and friends and shared occasionally in church meetings. Any formal elements, any use of rhythmic effects, is included to provide pleasant-sounding rhymes or to signal that the work is indeed poetry and therefore deserving of special attention and emotion.

In the past thirty years a new tradition of Mormon poetry has developed. It contains very few hymns, little narrative work, and tends, like most modern poetry, to renounce didacticism. The poets in this tradition are generally university-trained, many of them sympathetic to modern trends in literature and therefore interested in formal skill and experimentation. They tend to be ironic, intellectually playful, skeptical, self-reflexive, and—like their peers in mainstream American poetry—they have tended to move away from traditional forms and to feel some anxiety about whether language can really develop and communicate ideas and values. Yet, like their Mormon predecessors, they care deeply about ideas and values, even some extremely specific ones that they claim to know through religious experience, and they act with energy to communicate those ideas in confidence that they will be understood, at least by fellow Mormons.

It is this contemporary tradition from which we presume to collect this harvest. We believe the tradition can be usefully described and illustrated with good examples. The fifty-three poets included here have influenced each other in such ways that their work is mutually illuminating and cumulative in its delights and instruction. We believe that the tradition these works reveal and define is not only valuable in itself but different in important ways both from other Mormon artistic traditions and from other contemporary poetry.

These Mormon poets tend toward what in my view is an unusually healthy integration of skillful form with significant content. Though much Mormon poetry still continues to neglect form, most American poetry increasingly neglects content—ideas and values are negated or simply missing. For at least two hundred years, European and then American literary culture has increasingly lost confidence in Platonic realism, the possibility that language provides a bridge between the world and the human mind. During the last century poets have lost confidence in the traditional forms that were developed precisely to give language power to define the world in a systematic way. Increasingly, poetic form has become merely a demanding game to play with sounds and feelings—rather than, as it was for Chaucer and Shakespeare and still to some extent for Keats, an objective means of expressing meaning. Mormon poets in the tradition we present here tend to share modern anxieties and let their forms reflect the influences of developments in "free verse" and "minimalist"—even "nominalist" or "deconstructive"—writing that grows out of honest attention to their convictions about the subjective nature of language. But they also retain faith in its ability to communicate shared insights across time and space, based on their conviction that speech ultimately is connected both to the material universe and to our own minds because God is the creator of that universe and illuminates our minds. These poets, then, continue the ancient tradition of making rhythmic combinations of sounds to help readers discover a world that exists and can be defined by language, and to share insights into how to live better in that world.

In 1968 Karl Keller wrote in a review, "I think that at some far-distant point in time the history of Mormon poetry may well have to be said to have begun with Clinton F. Larson and this first collection of his verse, *The Lord of Experience*" (*Dialogue: A Journal of Mormon Thought*, Spring 1968). As Keller pointed out, Larson's first book was ground-breaking not because it was good poetry so much (though it was) as that it was the first Mormon poetry that was *real* poetry: "It does not show art filling a religious purpose but shows . . . religion succeeding in an esthetic way." Influenced by his teacher at the University of Utah, the fine modern poet Brewster Ghiselin, as well as by the poetry of T. S. Eliot, Larson was the first Mormon to make poetry his religious vocation, the means to observe and understand better his own people, their history, faith, and divine potential.

Larson was different from the first generation of Mormon writers, who used poetry to attack Babylon, the world they had renounced, and to defend Zion, which they had given everything to find and build. He was thus quite different from the tradition of home literature published in the church magazines and in a few books by the church press. But Larson was also unlike the first well educated and "modern" generation of Mormon writers, the regionalists of the 1930s and 1940s, who attained a national audience for "coming of age" fiction that attacked Mormon materialism, authoritarianism, anti-intellectualism, and cultural provinciality.

Instead, Larson developed, essentially without models or sympathetic peers, a poetry of deep but critical faith, able both to attack and affirm the world, Mormon history, and Mormon faith. And he did all this with great and developing poetic skill as well as the intellectual and emotional power sufficient to energize his formal achievements. A primary example of this is what I consider Larson's finest poem, "To a Dying Girl," a perfect jewel of a modern Mormon lyric because it uses subtly varied traditional form to create precise understanding and proper emotional response to an important idea about the tragic claims of mortality in the face of sincere faith in immortality.

Larson began writing in the early 1950s, but it was not until the 1960s, when he began publishing regularly in *Brigham Young University Studies*, which he helped found in 1959, and *Dialogue: A Journal of Mormon Thought*, which began in 1966, that he started to influence those who helped him establish the modern Mormon poetic tradition. Of course, others had been writing good poetry — such as Edward Hart and Marden Clark, his colleagues at Brigham Young University, and Veneta Nielson, active in the Utah Poetry Society — and some of that work could be called "Mormon" because of its religious or regional content. But Larson was the first to write consistently and openly, as well as skillfully and subtly, from the position of his deeply felt Mormon Christian faith. Many others were greatly influenced, not so much by his style or even subject matter as by a new possibility — poetry that was both Mormon and honestly reflective of personal feelings, rather than institutional needs.

Of course, most others, though "liberated" by Larson, developed their own voices and made unique contributions: Hart wrote first-rate hymns and ultimately produced a more unified book of poems in *To Utah* (1980) — a complete poetic and religious pilgrimage — than Larson or anyone else has thus far. John Sterling Harris focused on more traditional Western themes in his book *Barbed Wire* (1975), Marden Clark on more obviously personal and family subjects in *Moods, of Late* (1980). Carol Lynn Pearson, in a series of popular, nationally anthologized collections, developed a unique combination of traditional Mormon didacticism and clever turns of phrases and rhyming. Emma Lou Thayne, working as a student and teacher at the University of Utah, began like Pearson but quickly developed a powerful voice that moved into both experimental forms and wider subject matter — from the personal and familial to war, ecology, Israel, and cultural and generational relationships. Mary Bradford and Robert A. Rees, who served as *Dialogue*'s second and third editors in the 1970s and continued to promote the new tradition by publishing poetry regularly and editing special literary issues of the journal, also contributed occasionally to the new tradition with their own skillful personal lyrics.

Some of the poets included here came into the tradition from outside the Mormon faith or Utah culture, bringing challenging and enriching perspectives and forms. Arthur Henry King, a British convert who was a friend of T. S.

Eliot, brings to bear an already mature modern style on his exciting discoveries in the Mormon past and theology and some disappointing trends in the Mormon present. R. A. Christmas, a back-sliding convert from California, provides sometimes funky, always highly-crafted ruminations on his continuing pilgrimage of faith and renewal. Vernice Pere, a convert of Polynesian ancestry widely published in Hawaii, brings to the Mormon tradition a challenging devotion to her own culture. Donnell Hunter and Ronald Wilcox, never part of the Wasatch Front culture, speak of Mormon and Western things with unusual, somewhat sharper voices.

Besides Harris, two poets who have powerfully conveyed the Great Basin, high desert, Mormon experience are Karl Sandberg and David L. Wright. Wright died of a heart attack at age 38 in 1967, leaving impressive achievements in short story and drama and a long narrative poem, *River Saints*, which is unique in its bardic voice and effective portrayal of small-town Mormonism. But most of the poetry in this new Mormon tradition, in keeping with the concurrent development of Mormonism from a Western American to a world religion, is independent of the West and the formative pioneering experience. It speaks from specific locations around the world—a New England graveyard, the beach at Del Mar, a New Zealand hillside. And it speaks about universal concerns— temporary remission of cancer, raising children, the conflict of cultures in oneself—in a diversity of voices, but all of them in their own way Mormon.

Editors' Commentary

New Directions

DENNIS CLARK

Occasionally, when Mormon writers and readers get together and talk over things mainly of interest to themselves, one of them will ask if there truly is, or can be, a distinctively "Mormon" literature. I have made that mistake. I have even been so rude as to insist on pursuing the specific question, "Is there a Mormon poetry?" We ask ourselves such questions partly because we fear no one else is asking them, and believe that *someone* should. We are usually asking: "Is there a body of writing by Mormons which we should be studying for its literary value?" for most of us doing the asking are academics.

To that question, I have found only one answer: "Is there a Mormon audience for poetry?" This anthology gathers recent poems by Mormons. Rather than attempt to answer the first question, or provide grist for the second, it tests the third. If there is no Mormon audience for poetry, the work represented here will remain a minor sport of the American poetry whence it was gleaned.

The matter of audience is important: of all arts, literature is most social, its medium most fully the property of its audience. Virtually everyone talks, whether or not they can sing, whistle, dance, paint or form an ashtray with their face in wet clay. Unlike painting and sculpture, literature must be performed to be appreciated. But unlike music, drama and dance, it can be comfortably performed by its audience alone. It is, in fact, the only art whose audience *must be* its performers. For lovers of literature, even a reading by the author is not enough. The reader wants to enjoy the work by herself, for itself.

This is usually a solitary pleasure. One performs, say, a novel in relative silence and isolation, shutting everything else out to live the story. This shouldn't be the case with a poem. Although it can certainly be studied in silence, a poem can only be *enjoyed* in full voice. One must speak a poem to perform it; one must hear a poem to receive it. In this regard, as in the matter of time, poetry is more akin to music than the novel. Just as the score of a sonata is not its music, so the printed poem is not its poetry. The page holds what the poet wants you to say, what you want to hear.

Poetry takes as its medium not text but the sounds of language. Poets compose to be *heard*. To that end, they use a tongue common to an entire people. Once having made of that speech something they believe to be beautiful, they want to make it public, give it back to their friends for their pleasure. For *your* pleasure, I urge you to read these poems aloud.

None of my assertions about the aural nature of poetry is unique to me, or new. But an awareness of them is flooding back into American verse, modifying the "modern poetry" which Gene rightly identifies as the source of his new tradition. This awareness of sound verse erupted for many readers in an article by Frederick Turner and Ernst Pöppel, entitled "The Neural Lyre: Poetic Meter, the Brain, and Time" published in the August 1983 issue of *Poetry*. The authors argue, on the basis of recent studies in neuroanatomy and the physiology of the brain, and by analogy with Noam Chomsky's work on syntactical subordination, that there are universals in poetry which can be traced to the structure of the brain: it is made in units, "lines," which take about three seconds to recite (thus line length is a function of speech, not typography); certain elements of the language repeat among the lines (rhyme the most obvious); and well-made verse features variation.

For those reasons, and at the risk of disagreeing with Gene, I believe that the content of a poem is secondary to its sound. Reading a poem without moving your lips is like eating without tasting your food—regardless of what the food "means." The elements of verse that contribute to the taste of a poem are largely phonetic rather than semantic; the sounds, rather than what they mean. Moreover, much of our pleasure in a poem comes from the careful integration of its grammatical structure with the rhythmic structure, or meter, of the verse. That is so because of the nature of language. It is the first talent a child develops toward being human, and the foundation for all others. Learning one's native tongue is a major intellectual achievement, which the child masters by about five, before any formal schooling. And the same elements that so delight the learning child—the sounds, the rhymes, the consonance and assonance and dissonance of sound clusters, rhythmic chants and breaths, puns and wordplay—are what make good verse. People want to hear verse and to recite it because they have an inborn *need* to use language, manifest at birth. Verse concentrates language at its best. It is literal food for the spirit.

That's why people will gladly quote even a bad poem in Sacrament meeting, rather than try to say the same thing in their own words—not for the message, but because they find the poem beautiful, regardless of how stupid it might be. Only ignorance of good verse, only not knowing well-written poems in their own language, leads people to settle for the likes of Edgar A. Guest. And it is in their own language, the one they learned, the one they speak, that they want poems.

As for the subjects of these poems, not all are related to Mormon experience. When I answered the question "Is there a Mormon poetry?" with the question "Is there a Mormon audience for poetry?" I left off the last half of the answer: "For there are good poems being written by Mormons." But are the poems themselves good Mormons? Phrased that way, the question of subject matter seems as irrelevant as that of type-face—if marginally more interesting.

What I am promoting here is a distinction between verse as a medium of expression, and poetry as an expression of feeling. In general, I have chosen for this anthology not poetry, but fiction in verse. If the poem is written in careful and elegant verse as an act of fiction, the poetry will be there to feed the reader. We prepare food not only for bulk, nutrition and appearance, but for taste. The taste of a poem is as elusive as the taste of food—and fully as important to our enjoyment of it.

I find a love of language in these poems. I also find in all of them a commitment to fiction. Like other modes of discourse, such as analysis, description and interpretation, fiction can be written in verse or prose. Verse fiction takes the form of the poem. Its subject may be very "unpoetic" and still succeed. Milton wrote a sonnet, a love-poem, on the slaughter of Protestants in the Piedmont. With this odd combination, he made the matter new for the reader. New stories of our lives, compressed, polished, sculpted for our tongues — these are what we hope for. In a poem, much more than in a novel, I want the language of the story to delight me, however much the subject might appall.

The only criterion of less value to me than subject matter in determining the quality of a poem is message, and the two are wed. If the writer had wanted to push a message, he would've written an essay or bought an ad. A poem is the product of a poet's need to speak and the audience's need to hear. I do not assert with this strange idea that message is of no importance to a poem; what a poem says is second only to how it is said. But the message is so conditioned on the poet's command of language that, if the metrics and phonetics of the poem are slighted, it will be harder for the poet to write well than for a rock star to avoid dippy rhymes. In fact, if nothing else were available as evidence of the irrelevance of message to poetry, the popularity of rock lyrics among a wide segment of the populace would do.

And some of the poetry of the younger poets here reads as if it were modeled on rock lyrics. Much of it is written in present-tense, first-person narration. I dislike present-tense verse, finding it ineffective; it seems intended (and it is widely used by American poets, and Mormon poets, today) to describe a static or near-static scene. It becomes monotonous, even toneless, almost as if used to damp your emotional response. There is little awareness of history behind such flat verse, and little concern for the world. What awareness there is shows itself in poems about grandparents, or ancestors. But that bothers me less than bad-sounding verse, because I believe that the subject matter, like the meaning, is of secondary interest in a poem.

That's because what survives in a body of poetry often means something entirely different to those who continue to read than it meant to the generation that produced it. And this anthology is no exception. *The audience of a poem determines, to a greater extent than its author, what a poem means.* It is their language he has used to make the poem. Only if the poem enters into that language will it have any meaning; only if it gives back to the speakers of that language some of the beauty and joy language first gave them, some of the playfulness, some of the fun, some of the truth.

Notes on Poets, and Acknowledgements

The names of Utah cities, and major cities elsewhere, are given without the state; names of Utah universities are abbreviated (with "University" always shortened to "U."). Titles marked with an asterisk (*) are reprinted here from the source listed. Poems in this anthology not listed below the author's name are published here for the first time. The section "Hymns and Songs" includes the following texts from *Hymns of the Church of Jesus Christ of Latter-day Saints* (Salt Lake City: Church of Jesus Christ of Latter-day Saints, 1985), which are reprinted by permission: "We Meet Again As Sisters," by Paul L. Anderson (p. 253); "Each Life that Touches Ours for Good," by Karen Lynn Davidson (p. 256); "I Know My Father Lives," by Reid N. Nibley, copyright 1969 (p. 262); "Bless Our Fast, We Pray," by John S. Tanner (p. 263); and "Teach Me to Walk in the Light," by Clara W. McMaster (p. 262). Other selections from *1985 Hymns* are acknowledged below with the poet's other work and are reprinted by permission.

The following bibliographies are not complete, but are intended to help the reader find representative poems we were not able to include as well as acknowledge prior publication of those we did and point out important reviews and critical essays. For many citations, we have relied on information from contributors and cannot guarantee that all citations are completely accurate. We have used short titles for magazines well-known to readers of Mormon literature: *BYU Studies* refers to *Brigham Young University Studies*; *Dialogue* to *Dialogue: A Journal of Mormon Thought*; *Ensign* to *The Ensign of the Church of Jesus Christ of Latter-day Saints*; and *Sunstone* to *Sunstone: A ... Journal of Mormon Experience, Issues, Essays and Art*. *Wye, Century II*, and *Inscape* are or were literary magazines of Brigham Young University, and *Kula Manu* is a literary magazine of Brigham Young University-Hawaii. In addition, the anthology *Poems of Praise*, eds. Edward L. Hart and Marden J. Clark (Provo, UT: College of Humanities of Brigham Young University, 1980), is cited by title only, and without page number(s), as are *22 Young Mormon Writers*, eds. Neal E. Lambert and Richard H. Cracroft (Provo, UT: Communications Workshop, 1975), and Cracroft and Lambert's *A Believing People: Literature of the Latter-day Saints* (Provo, UT: Brigham Young University Press, 1974). Prizes awarded by the Association for Mormon Letters are cited as "AML prize"; those by the Utah Arts Council in its Original Writing contest as "Utah Arts Council prize."

PENNY ALLEN P. 124

Raised in Castro Valley and San Jose, California, Allen attended San Jose State and BYU, earning a B.A. at the former and an M.A. at the latter. She has produced two novels, the text of a cantata, myriad poems, and two hymns appearing in the 1985 LDS hymnal.

*"I Will One Day Be a Widow, Love." *Exponent II* 5.3 (1979).
*"Post Partum Blues." *Exponent II* 6.4 (1980).
*"Blackberry." *Sunstone* 10.10 (1986).

★"The Coyote." *Sunstone* 11.1 (1987).
★"The Word was Unperfected Till Made Flesh" and ★"Tefnut" (accepted for *Sunstone*).

KATHRYN R. ASHWORTH   P. 254

A native of Moab, Ashworth graduated from BYU in 1963 in French and English. She has taught French at the U. of Oklahoma and lives in Provo, where she composes hymns and writes poems. She is at work on a series of poems relating to Mormon church history.
"Patterns of Light and Shadow." *Mountainwest Magazine*, Feb. 1977.
"Toward Manti." *BYU Studies* 17.2 (1977).
"Elegy for Leslie, a Thirteen-Year-Old Girl." *Ensign*, June 1979.
"At My Daughter's Baptism." *Ensign*, March 1980.
"Three Cathedrals in Spain: Toledo, Barcelona and Leon." *Dialogue* 13.3 (1980).
"A Letter to My Husband." *Poems of Praise.*
"Jochebed and the Nile." *Ensign*, March 1982.
"November Second." *Rocky Mountain Review of Language & Literature* 39.1 (1985).
"Rocky Mountain Modern Language Association Convention: Glendale, Arizona." *Gila Review* [2 (1985)].
★"A Weathered Cross Beside the Wall." *Sunstone* 11.3 (1987).
"Young Hawks." *BYU Today* 41.4 (1987). 1st place, Chair Competition, 1986 Eisteddfod, BYU.

DANIELLE BEAZER   P. 241

Raised in Charlottesville, Virginia, Beazer earned a B.A. in English in 1985 from BYU, spent two years teaching and freelancing in Boston, received her M.A. in English and Creative Writing from Stanford in 1989 and is now teaching at BYU.
★"An Awakening." *Tar River Poetry* 25.2 (1986).
★"The Next Day" and "Women Friends." *Inscape*, Winter 1986.
★"Over the Other Side of the Country" and "This, the Summer." *Inscape*, Winter 1987.

ELOUISE BELL   P. 94

Perhaps best known for her humorous writing in her column "Only When I Laugh," which appears in *Network*, Bell has taught many BYU students to laugh with her, sometimes at the most painful things. She is completing a young adult novel and planning publication of a collection of essays.
"The Prodigal's Mother." *BYU Studies* 19.4 (1979).
★"Psalm for a Saturday Night." *Poems of Praise.*
★"This Do in Remembrance of Me." *Ensign*, April 1980.

MARY BLANCHARD   P. 197

Blanchard, a mother of four, has a B.A. in English from the U. of Utah. She is presently working on an M.A. in creative writing at California State U., Sacramento, having also worked as an editor, a teacher and a writer. She has published essays, short stories, and poetry.
"The Veil." *Exponent II* 5.3 (1979).
"Jonestown I." *Exponent II* 6.1 (1979).

MARY LYTHGOE BRADFORD   P. 61

A graduate of the U. of Utah with degrees in Education and English (and a thesis on Mormon novelists), Bradford is a writer, editor, and teacher. She edited *Dialogue* from 1977 to 1982, and has compiled two collections of essays, as well as a book of her own essays. She is currently writing a biography of Lowell Bennion.
"Joseph," ★"Advice," and "The Difference." *Dialogue* 1.3 (1966).
"Cat." *The Evening Star*, 4 March 1966.
"Regretfully Request," "Letting Go," "Buffers," and "Heritage." *BYU Studies* 9.4 (1969).
"The Beautiful." *The Carpenter* 1.4 (1969-71).
★"Triad" and "Holy Thursday." *Dialogue* 6.2 (1971).
"The Grammarian Blows Her Mind." *Dialogue* 10.2 (1975).
"My Childhood Calls Me." *Ensign*, April 1977.
★"Coming Apart Together." *Exponent II* 9.1 (1982).
★"Born Again." *Dialogue* 17.3 (1984).
Leaving Home: A Collection of Personal Essays. Salt Lake City: Signature, 1987. AML essay prize, 1988.

MARILYN MCMEEN BROWN   P. 111; P. 255

Since writing her first novel as a ten-year-old in Denver, Brown has filled many pages with verse and prose. Originally a music student at BYU, she gravitated from flute to pen, a change producing the novels *The Earthkeepers* and *House on the Sound* (forthcoming U. of Utah Press).
★"Indian Playmate." *Rainflowers*. Provo: Art Publishers, 1969. "New Express" reprinted in *A Believing People*.
★"Grandmother" and ★"Will you Remember?" *The Grandmother Tree*. Provo: Art Publishers, 1978.
★"Thy Servants Are Prepared." *1985 Hymns*.

R. A. CHRISTMAS   P. 128

Educated at Stanford (A.B. 1961), Berkeley (A.M. 1963), and U.S.C. (Ph.D. 1968), Christmas taught English at Idaho State, U.S.C., San Jose State, and

Southern Utah State College (where he served as department chair). He left teaching in 1973 to pursue a career in business, and is still writing.
"To Joseph Smith." *BYU Studies* 6.1 (1964).
"At Temple Square, Salt Lake City." *Dialogue* 1.3 (1966).
"The Convert: 1957." *The Southern Review* 4.1 (1968).
"A Translation of Paul Valery's 'Ebauche d'un Serpent.'" *Dialogue* 3.1 (1968).
"Theater of the Absurd." *Anomaly: The San Jose Quarterly Review*, Fall 1968.
★"At Mountain Meadows, Utah," "Adam," and "Eve." *Dialogue* 4.3 (1969). Reprinted in *A Believing People*.
★"Driving Without Lights" [reprinted as "In Beaver Canyon"]. *The Southern Review* 6.2 (1970): 447-48.
"Rodney the Raper." *Western Humanities Review* 26.2 (1972).
"John D. Lee" *Dialogue* 7.2 (1972).
★"Ghost Truck." *Dialogue* 7.3 (1972).
"Looking West from Cedar City, Utah." *Dialogue* 8.3-4 (1973).
"Playing Softball Against the Polygamists." *Sunstone* 10.6 (1985).
★"Self-portrait as Brigham Young." *Sunstone* 11.4 (1987). AML prize, 1988.

DENNIS CLARK   P. 163

Clark works at Orem Public Library, and as the poetry editor for *Sunstone*. He also publishes poetry chapbooks under various imprints.
"Corn Grows in Rows." *Dialogue* 5.2 (1970).
"A Name and a Blessing." *Dialogue* 5.3 (1970).
"Statement Before the World Expands." *Dialogue* 6.3-4 (1971).
"Meadow." *Dialogue* 8.2 (1973). Reprinted in *A Believing People*.
"Knifing a Piggy Bank." *Poetry Northwest* 18.2 (1977).
"American Neanderthal." *Exponent II* 5.1 (1978).
"Before the World Expands." *Dialogue* 11.3 (1978).
★"Song for His Left Ear." *Dialogue* 12.4 (1979).
"Poets in Praise of God." Rev. of *Voices Within the Ark: the Modern Jewish Poets*, ed. Howard Schwartz and Anthony Rudolph. *The Sunstone Review* 2.2 (1982).
"Stealing Roses." *Exponent II* 8.2 (1982).
"Poetry as Fiction." Rev. of Dave Smith, *Dream Flights: Poems. The Sunstone Review* 2.8 (1982).
"The New Mormon Poetry." Rev. of Lewis Horne, *The Seventh Day. Dialogue* 17.1 (1984).
"The Old Mormon Poetry." Rev. of Carol Lynn Pearson, *The Widening View. Dialogue* 17.4 (1984).
"Mormon poetry: the state of the art." [4 articles] *Sunstone*. Part 1: 10.6 (1985); Part 2: 10.10 (1986); Part 3: 11.1 (1987); Part 4: (scheduled, 1989).
"Sunwatch." *Literature and Belief* 6 (1986). AML prize, 1987.
★"New Name and Blessing." *BYU Studies* 26.3 (1986).

★"On the Stranding of Great Whales." *Tinder: dry poems*. Orem: Salt the Lake, 1988. AML prize, 1989.

MARDEN J. CLARK   P. 15

Raised on a farm in Morgan, Clark has been a trucker, worked for Lockheed, and taught English at BYU, where he started writing poetry. Retired, he is assembling a book of poems, *Razor Sharp*, and working on an autobiography.
★"To Kevin: Newly a Missionary" and ★"Wasatch." *Moods, Of Late*. Provo: BYU Press, 1979. AML Prize, 1980, for *Moods, of Late*.
★"August 6." *Dialogue* 21.2 (1988).
★"Joseph's Christmas Eve." *Christmas Voices*. Orem: Balanced Books, 1988.

IRIS PARKER CORRY   P. 26

Awarded first prize in the Utah Fine Arts writing contest for serious poetry (1977), Corry is now retired.
"November Freeze" and "The Day President Harding Came." *Dialogue* 8.3–4 (1973).
★"Nellie Unthank" and ★"The Year of the Famine." *Bread and Milk for Supper*. Cedar City: I. P. Corry, 1987.

JOHN DAVIES   P. 267

Davies lives with his wife and daughter in Prestatyn, Wales, where he teaches English. He has taught at the U. of Michigan and U. of Washington, and was visiting professor of poetry at BYU, 1987–88.
The Visitor's Book. Poetry Wales Press, 1986. Won Alice Hunt Bartlett Prize from the British Poetry Society.
★"What Doesn't End When the Year Ends" (accepted for *Tar River Poetry*).
★"For the Welsh Mormons" (accepted for *Planet*).
★"Driving the Provo River" (accepted for *New Mexico Humanities Review*).

COLIN B. DOUGLAS   P. 157

Brought up on Puget Sound, Douglas spent two years at the U. of Washington before earning a B.S. in psychology and an M.A. in English at BYU. He has worked in military intelligence and news reporting, and is currently an editor for the LDS church.
"I Sought Thee, Adonai." *Ensign*, Oct. 1979.
★"Take, Eat" and "Wedding Song." *Dialogue* 13.4 (1980).
"Mine Beyond Death: Doctrine and Covenants 132." *Ensign*, Feb. 1981.
"A Daughter of Sarah is My Beloved." *Sunstone* 8.6 (1983).
★"Wedding Songs," ★"Adonai: Cover Me," and "As Shaddai Descends." *Sunstone* 10.10 (1986).
"Haiku." *Dragonfly: East/West Haiku Quarterly* 13.2 (1985).

"Haiku." *Dragonfly: East/West Haiku Quarterly* 13.3 (1985).
"Adoni: I Have Sinned" and "Adoni: Forsake Me Not." *Sunstone* 12.1 (1988).

EUGENE ENGLAND   P. 78

Raised in Downey, Idaho, and Salt Lake City, England moved to California to study at Stanford, where he helped found *Dialogue* in 1966 and received a Ph.D. in 1974. He teaches American and Mormon literature, Shakespeare, and creative writing at BYU.
★"The Temenos" and "The Classic Angler." *The Southern Review* N S 1.1 (1965).
"The Firegiver." *Dialogue* 1.1 (1966).
"Charlotte's Cadenza." *Exponent II* 6.2 (1980); reprinted 10.4 (1984).
★"Sunrise on Christmas." *Ensign*, Dec. 1979.
"Black Walnut." *Literature and Belief* 1 (1981).
★"My Kinsman." [Published as "Kinsman."] *BYU Studies* 21.4 (1981).
"Making the Porch." *BYU Studies* 23.2 (1983).
★"Cri du Chat." *Literature and Belief* 3 (1983). Winner in Christian Values Writing Contest.
★"Pilgrims." 1st Place, Crown Competition, 1989 Eisteddfod, BYU.

KATHY EVANS   P. 171

Evans grew up in a small Utah steel-making town. She attended Northwestern, the U. of Utah, and San Francisco State, earning an M.A. in Broadcast Communication in 1980. She began teaching with California Poets-in-the-Schools in 1981.
"Journey into Morning" and "Pale Woman, Lean Woman." *Ensign*, March 1980.
"At Richardson's Bay." *The Pacific Sun*, May 1980.
"Lines Loose at Midnight." *The California Quarterly*, Fall 1983.
★"Handwritten Psalm." *Deep Valley Review* 3 (Spring 1984).
"Unfinished Sestina for the Secretary of Defense." *Dialogue* 17.4 (1984).
"Returning." *Dialogue* 18.1 (1985).
"For the Bishop's Wife." *Dialogue* 19.2 (1986).
"Tomorrow." *The Marin Review*, Summer 1986.
"Dorothy Picks Up Two Hitchhikers" and "Spring Ode for Aphrodite." *The Berkeley Review* 20 (Fall 1986).
"Nativity." *Dialogue* 19.4 (1986).
"Knocking." *Occident* 102.1 (1987).
"Here's the Church." *Dialogue* 21.4 (1988).

BREWSTER GHISELIN   P. 270

Born in Missouri, Ghiselin studied at UCLA, Berkeley, and Oxford before settling in Utah to teach at the U. of Utah. His published works include the landmark compilation, *The Creative Process.*

Against the Circle. New York: E. P. Dutton, 1946.
The Creative Process: A Symposium. Berkeley: U. of California Press, 1952; reprinted in 1985.
The Nets. New York: E. P. Dutton, 1955.
Country of the Minotaur. Salt Lake City: U. of Utah Press, 1970.
The Water of Light: A Miscellany in Honor of Brewster Ghiselin. Ed. Henry Taylor. Salt Lake City: U. of Utah Press, 1976.
Light. Omaha: U. of Nebraska, 1978.
★"Rattlesnake" and ★"A View of Little Scope." *Windrose: Poems 1929–1979.* Salt Lake City: U. of Utah Press, 1980. Reprinted by permission. *Windrose* won the Poetry Society of America's William Carlos Williams Award in 1981.
★"Fragment." *Literature and Belief* 6 (1986).

STEPHEN GOULD   P. 152

Raised in Fairfield/Suisun, California, Gould earned a B.A. at BYU and an M.A. in English at the U. of Utah.
"The New Covenant." *Dialogue* 1.1 (1966).
"Zenith Landing" and "To the Desert's Eye." *Dialogue* 9.1 (1974).
★"Fish Census" and ★"Tribunal Alien." *Sunstone* 4.1 (1979).
★Group Session." *Sunstone* 6.3 (1981).
"The Corner Window." *Sunstone* 7.1 (1982).
"To Silence." *Sunstone* 10.6 (1985).
★"Sabbath Flower." *Sunstone* 10.10 (1986).
"Difficulty at the Beginning." *Sunstone* 11.3 (1987).

STEVEN WILLIAM GRAVES   P. 175

A native of Salt Lake City, Graves earned a B.A. at the U. of Utah, studied at the U. of Kiel, and earned an M.Phil. and Ph.D. at Yale. He is presently an instructor in medicine at Harvard Medical School and an administrator at the Brigham and Women's Hospital.
"snow." *Folio* 6.1 (1970).
"Dido." *Cimmarron Review,* July 1970.
"Blackberries" and "Storm at Dawn." *Wasatch Front* 58.2 (1970).
"Rosary" and "Seven." *Florida Quarterly* 4.2 (1972).
"Imaginary Letters to a Friend." *Western Humanities Review* 27.2 (1973).
"The Rendezvous." *Poetry: Points of Departure.* Ed. by Henry Taylor. Cambridge, Mass.
"Ivory Spheres in a Chinese Carving." *Poetry,* Dec. 1976.
★"Early Invitations." *The Yale Review,* March 1977.
"Deportment in Ropes." *The New Journal* 10.2 (1977).
★"The Cancellation" and "Small Anthem." *Poetry,* Oct. 1977.
"The Augury." *Shenandoah* 30.2 (1978).
"The Graveyard of Small Children." *Kansas Quarterly* 2.1–2 (1979).

"The Room of Facing Mirrors." *Dialogue* 13.3 (1980).

RANDALL L. HALL   P. 181

Although born in Logan, Hall spent his childhood in central California before moving back to Utah, to Mantua. He lives now in Orem and is manager of seminary curriculum for the LDS church.

"From Branch of Willow," "A Paper Afternoon," and "Concerning One Older." *Utah Sings* 1974.

"Water From a Basin." *Ensign*, March 1978.

"To See Thy Face." *BYU Studies* 19.4 (1979).

Mosaic. Salt Lake City: Utah State Poetry Society, 1979.

★"Passover: a Mirrored Epiphany." *Dialogue* 14.3 (1981).

"Autumn Garden." *Deseret News*, 11 Nov. 1981.

"The Bier of Autumn." *BYU Studies* 22.4 (1982).

"Saints and Dancers." *BYU Studies* 23.2 (1983).

"Repapering the Kitchen." *Dialogue* 16.2 (1983).

"The Taciturn Phylactery." *BYU Studies* 23.4 (1983).

"The Kindling of Souls." *Deseret News*, 17 Sep. 1986.

"Gadfield Elm Chapel," "The Bells of Malvern," and "Seeds of Fire." *BYU Studies* 27.2 (1987).

★"The Apogee of Loneliness" accepted for *BYU Studies*.

LAURA HAMBLIN   P. 229

A long-time resident of Provo, Hamblin has earned an Associate Degree in Nursing (RN), a B.A. in English and philosophy, and an M.A. in English from BYU. She is presently writing children's stories for IBM.

"Their Grandmothers." *Exponent II* 12.4 (1986).

"The Molting Season." *Exponent II* 13.1 (1986).

★"From the Next Weird Sister," "Palenque," and "The Molting Season." *Inscape*, Winter 1987.

★"The Next Weird Sister Attempts Repentance." *Sunstone* 12.2 (1988).

"A.M. Revelation." *BYU Studies* 28.2 (1988).

"Palenque." *Sunstone* 13.2 (1989).

"Frogs in Paria Canyon" and "The Next Weird Sister Loses Weight." *Inscape* 1989, v. 1.

★"Divorce" and "Lindon Cannery, November 12, 1982." *Dialogue* 22.3 (1989).

"To Baptize" accepted for *Midland Review*.

"Unto Tarshish" accepted for *BYU Studies*.

JOHN STERLING HARRIS   P. 45

A teacher of English at BYU, Harris has written poetry and books on technical writing. He has completed a second volume of poems, *An Age of Wonders*.

★"E. H. 1817" and ★"Apprentice." *Poems of Praise.*
★"Fallow." *Dialogue* 7.3 (1972).
★"Tag, I.D." *Listen, the War: Poetry of the Viet Nam War.* Eds., Fredrick Kiley and Anthony Dater. Boulder, CO: USAF Academy Press, 1973. Reprinted in *Barbed Wire.*
★"Hay Derrick." *Barbed Wire.* Provo: BYU Press, 1974. This and "The Assassination of Emma Gray" reprinted in *A Believing People.*
"Flight." 2d place, Chair Competition, 1986 Eisteddfod, BYU.

EDWARD L. HART   P. 20; P. 257

Born in Bloomington, Idaho, Hart earned a B.S. in economics from U. of Utah, an M.A. in English from Michigan, and a D.Phil. from Oxford as a Rhodes Scholar.
★"To Utah," ★"Winter," ★"Spring," ★"The Gentle Way," and ★"The Launching." *To Utah.* Provo: BYU Press, 1979. AML Prize and Utah Arts Council 1st Prize.
★"Depletion." *BYU Studies* 21.4 (1981).
★"New York Provincial." *Mountainwest,* Sept. 1978.
★"Our Savior's Love." *1985 Hymns.*

LEWIS HORNE   P. 76

Born in Arizona, Horne earned a B.A. at Arizona State and an M.A. and Ph.D. at the U. of Michigan. He has taught at Michigan, Colorado College, and the U. of Saskatchewan, where he still teaches English.
"A Mormon Piano Teacher Asks for a Blessing" and "After a Fine Sonata." *Tar River Poetry* 21.1 (1981).
The Seventh Day. Saskatoon, Saskatchewan: Thistledown, 1982.
"Morning Thunder" and "Bus Terminal." *Ariel* 14.1 (1983).
"As When a Magic Broke." *Cumberland Poetry Review* 2.1 (1983).
"After Noon." *The Texas Review* 4.1–2 (1983).
"The Bottom Field" and "Moment of Confusion." *Cumberland Poetry Review* 3.2 (1983).
"My Face Surprising," "Letter from Nga," and "Private Vision." *Ontario Review* 19 (Fall-Winter 1983–84).
"Before the Wreckers Come" and "Irrigating." *Cumberland Poetry Review* 3.2 (1984).
"I Stood on the Beach and Observed" and "Burning." *Contemporary Verse II* 8.2 (1984).
"Press." *Queen's Quarterly* 91.4 (1984).
"Man Holding Lettuce" and "The Shores of Spring." *The Fiddlehead* 142 (Winter 1984).
"Conundrums of Color," "Silent Things," and "Homage to G. G." *Poetry,* May 1985.

"Looking On." *Cumberland Poetry Review* 4.2 (1985).
"The Churchhouse." *The Texas Review* 6.1–2 (1985).
"Perceiving a Season" and "The Cry." *Cumberland Poetry Review* 5.1 (1985).
"Being — Not So Simply." *Tar River Poetry* 25.1 (1985).
"The Space Between" and "For a Nephew — and Grade II Dropout." *The Fiddlehead* 147 (Spring 1986).
"4th Avenue." *Quarry* 35.4 (1986).
"Bess's Husband," "North Alma School Road," and "Another Clarity." *Ontario Review* 24 (Spring-Summer 1986).
"Family Reunion," "Trails," and "Speaking in Tongues." *Cumberland Poetry Review* 6.2 (1987).
"January." *Wascana Review* 22.1 (1987).
"The Claims of Summer." *Queen's Quarterly* 94.1 (1987).

SUSAN HOWE   P. 193

Raised in Pleasant Grove, Utah, Howe earned a B.A. from BYU, an M.A. from the U. of Utah, and a Ph.D. from Denver U. She has lived in Washington, D.C., and Boston, where she edited for an academic journal and for Houghton Mifflin and served as the editor of *Exponent II*. She now teaches at BYU.
"Flowering." *Exponent II* 5.3 (1979).
"The Death of a Guppy." *Exponent II* 6.1 (1979).
"Snow Advice from the Basketball Coach." *Exponent II* 7.2 (1981).
"The Covenant." *Sunstone* 6.3 (1981).
"Transmutation." *Exponent II* 7.3 (1981).
"Wind." *Exponent II* 7.4 (1981).
★"*Summer Days*, a Painting by Georgia O'Keeffe." *Kansas Quarterly* 19.4 (1987).
"Why I am a Witch" accepted for *Kansas Quarterly*.

DONNELL HUNTER   P. 64; P. 259

A native of Rigby, Idaho, Hunter teaches English at Ricks College, Rexburg, Idaho. He has published over 230 poems in 95 magazines, and operates the Honeybrook Press.
★"How Glorious Is the Voice We Hear." Hymn performed Oct. 1973, Ricks College devotional assembly.
★"The Lure" and ★"Our Town." *The Frog in Our Basement*. Rexburg: Honeybrook Press, 1984.
★"Children of Owl" and ★"Porcupine." *Children of Owl*. Rexburg: Honeybrook Press, 1985.
At Fort Worden. Rexburg: Honeybrook Press, 1986.
★"Confessions of a Disbeliever," ★"When it Stopped Singing," and ★"Sabbatical." *Turkeys and Trees*. Rexburg: Honeybrook Press, 1987.
Songs of the River. Rexburg: Honeybrook Press, 1988.

"Annals of Natural History." 2d place, Crown Competition, 1989 Eisteddfod, BYU.

CLIFTON JOLLEY   P. 167

Jolley holds a Ph.D. in English from BYU. He has taught at BYU and BYU–Hawaii and in the LDS church seminary system, and currently owns a media production company.
★"Prophet" and "The Men of Huntsville." *Dialogue* 7.3 (1972).
★"Mr. Bojangles." *Dialogue* 9.1 (1974).
"Heritage." *A Believing People.*
"Mamo." *22 Young Mormon Writers.*
"Three foot shallows drowner." *Dialogue* 10.1 (1975–76).
"The Genealogist as Scourge." *Sunstone* 2.1 (1976).
"Triptych." *Sunstone* 2.1 (1977).
"Mystery: Above Florence." *Sunstone* 4.3 (1979).

BRUCE W. JORGENSEN   P. 160; P. 260

A native of Salina and intermittent resident of Ithaca, New York, Jorgensen currently teaches English at BYU.
" 'Imperceptive Hands': Some Recent Mormon Verse." *Dialogue* 5.4 (1970).
★"On Second West in Cedar City, Utah: Canticle for the Virgin." *Dialogue* 6.1 (1971).
★"Gathering Apples in First Snow." *Dialogue* 6.3–4 (1971).
"Incompletions for a Living Father." *Carolina Quarterly* 24.1 (1972).
★"Weight of Glory," "Opening Lunch on Getting to the Office," "Syllables for a January Thaw," and "For No Dreams." *Dialogue* 7.3 (1972).
"Near an Abandoned Canal Bridge in Southern Utah." *Dialogue* 8.2 (1973).
★"A Litany for the Dark Solstice." *BYU Today*, Dec. 1976.
★"For Bread and Breath of Life." *Ensign*, March 1977.
"In the Cold House." *Dialogue* 11.3 (1978).
"The Vocation of David Wright: An Essay in Analytic Biography." *Dialogue* 11.2 (1978).
★"The Light Come Down." *Sunstone* 4.3 (1979).
"Beginning to Bodysurf." *Kula Manu*, 1981.
"Poetry as Narrative . . . " Rev. of Dave Smith, *Goshawk, Antelope. The Sunstone Review* 2.8 (1982).
★"Friends: a Moral Song." *Literature and Belief* 2.
"Thinking of the End in Fire." *BYU Studies* 25.1 (1985).

PATRICIA GUNTER KARAMESINES   P. 221

Graduated from BYU with an M.A. in English in 1986, Karamesines studied English at Arizona for a year. She now teaches philosophy part time at BYU and is working on a collection of stories, *Old Woman and Others*.
★"Open Range, Wyoming." *Century II* 5.3 (1981).
"Concerning the Revelations of Heaven and Earth." *Sunstone* 7.5 (1982).
"The Pear Tree." 1st place, Crown Competition, 1987 Eisteddfod, BYU.

KARL KELLER   P. 83

Raised in Manti, Keller attended the U. of Utah and earned a Ph.D. at the U. of Minnesota. He taught American literature at California State University at San Diego, publishing books on Robinson Jeffers, Edward Taylor, and Emily Dickinson. He died in 1985.
★"Faith" and ★"Creation." *Dialogue* 1.2 (1966).
★"Manti Temple." *BYU Studies* 1.2 (1959–60).
"Pilgrimage of Awe." Rev. of Clinton F. Larson, *The Lord of Experience. Dialogue* 6.1 (1968).
★"My Children on the Beach at Del Mar." *Dialogue* 7.3 (1972).

ARTHUR HENRY KING   P. 10

Born in England, King studied literature at Cambridge and earned a doctorate in philology at the the U. of Lund in Sweden. After joining the LDS church, he became Professor of English at BYU in 1971. He is now working on a computerized stylistic approach to Shakespeare, and on a book of poems, *Unclean Lips*.
"Visit to a Cathedral After a Trip Around the World," "Hot weather in Tucson," and "The Right Size." *Dialogue* 4.3 (1969). "Hot Weather" reprinted in *A Believing People*.
"Winter Solstice." *Dialogue* 6.1 (1971).
★"Latter Days." *Dialogue* 6.3 (1971).
★"I Will Make Thee a Terror to Thyself." *Dialogue* 7.3 (1972).
"First Snow." *New Era*, March 1973.
"A Prophet is Dead; a Prophet Lives." *Dialogue* 8.3 (1973)
"September on Campus." *New Era*, Oct. 1973.
"To the Savior at Christmas and Always." *Ensign*, Dec. 1973.
"September the First, 1969." *Dialogue* 9.1 (1974).
Three poems. *BYU Studies* 14.2 (1974).
★"Hebrews 11: Strangers and Pilgrims." *Ensign*, Jan. 1976.
"Be Still." *Ensign*, Dec. 1976.
"The Field Behind Holly House." AML prize (1977).
"Beyond our Works and Days." *Ensign*, July 1977.
"Epithalamion." *Dialogue* 11.3 (1978).
"Entitlement" and "President Kimball at Mestre." *BYU Studies* 25.4 (1985).

"Nature and the Bourgeois Poet." *BYU Studies* 26.3 (1986).
"Isis Egypt-Bound." *BYU Studies* 26.4 (1986).
"Before a Journey" and "Snowdrops at Ditchley Park." *BYU Studies* 27.2 (1987).
★"Death is the Frame of Love." *BYU Studies* 28.2 (1988).
"From Spring to Main: The Poetry of Arthur Henry King." *Ensign*, June 1988. Includes "At One," "Death's Ecstacy," "His Love," "In Memoriam N. W. for J. W.," "My Conversion," "Ripening Apples," "Hymn," etc.

LANCE LARSEN   P. 233

Larsen has lived in Idaho, Colorado, and Utah, where he earned a B.A. and M.A. from BYU in English. Now a Ph.D. candidate in Literature and Creative Writing at the U. of Houston, he also holds an Ehrhardt Graduate Fellowship.
★"After Fishing." *Literature and Belief* 5.
"Gathering Apples" and "Buffalo." *New Era*, Aug. 1986.
"Elegy for Richard Coones," "Birds," "Making Fruit Salad," and "Annie." *Inscape*, Fall 1987.
"Honeydew" and "Elegy for Richard Coones." *Wisconsin Review* 22.1 (1987).
"In the Summer of Grace." 1st place, Chair competition, 1988 Eisteddfod, BYU.
"After Nine." *Midland Review* 4 (1988).
"Karsh." *Fine Madness* 5.1 (1988).
"Moon." *The Literary Review* 31.3 (1988).
★"Passing the Sacrament at Eastgate Nursing Home." *BYU Studies* 27.4 (1987).
"In the Summer of Grace." 1st place, Chair Competition, 1988 Eisteddfod, BYU.
★"Dreaming Among Hydrangeas" accepted for *Apalachee Quarterly*.
"Walking to an Empty House" accepted for *BYU Studies*.
★"Light" accepted for *Literature and Belief*.

CLINTON F. LARSON   P. 28

Larson's poetry reflects a broad interest in all things human, cosmic, universal, and divine. A graduate of the U. of Denver, he was poet-in-residence at BYU at the time of his retirement in 1985.
The Mantle of the Prophet, and Other Plays. Salt Lake City: Deseret Book, 1966.
The Lord of Experience. Provo: BYU Press, 1967. Reviewed in *Dialogue* 3.1 (1968).
"A Conversation with Clinton Larson." *Dialogue* 4.3 (1969).
"A Letter from Israel Whiton," "Advent," "The Witness," and "Grandaughter" reprinted in *A Believing People*.
Counterpoint. Provo: BYU Press, 1973. Reviewed in *Dialogue* 9.1 (1974).
Schwartz, Thomas D. "Sacrament of Terror: Violence in the Poetry of Clinton F. Larson." *Dialogue* 9.3 (1974).

Modern Poetry of Western America. Ed. with William Stafford. Provo: BYU Press, 1975.
★"Lovers at Twilight." *The Western World.* Provo: Research Division, BYU, 1978.
Perry, Dennis. "Clinton F. Larson's 'The Witness'" The Quest for a Mormon Mythic Consciousness." M.A. Thesis, BYU, 1981.
"Romaunt of the Rose: A Tapestry of Poems by Clinton F. Larson." *BYU Studies* 23.1 (1983). AML prize.
★"Advent," ★"To a Dying Girl," ★"Jesse," ★"Arab Insurrection: a Memoir," and ★"Homestead in Idaho." *Selected Poems of Clinton F. Larson.* Ed. David L. Evans. Provo: BYU, 1988. AML special citation.
★"The Death of Ramses II." In "The Egyptian Poems," *BYU Studies* 26.4 (1986).
"The Civil War Poems." *BYU Studies* 28.4 (1988).

TIMOTHY LIU   P. 245

Liu was raised in San Jose, California, and is currently a graduate student in creative writing at U. of Houston, where he holds an Ehrhardt Graduate Fellowship. While at BYU, he served as editor of *Inscape*, won the Eisteddfod Chair and Mayhew contests, and received honorable mention from the Utah Fine Arts Council.
★"Death Calls." *Inscape*, Spring-Summer 1988.
"The Heat." *Inscape*, [Winter] 1988.
"So Cal." *Gridlock: an Anthology of Southern California Poetry.* Long Beach: Applezaba Press, 1989.
"Her Body." *BYU Studies* 27.3 (1987).
"Bittersweet." *BYU Studies* 27.4 (1987).
★"Cathedral" and ★"Paper Flowers." *A Zipper of Haze.* Orem: Winepress, 1988.
"Sonnets from Xian." 1st place, Chair Competition, 1989 Eisteddfod, BYU.
"Two Fishermen in Hong Kong" and "The Lord's Table." *Dialogue* 22.2 (1989).
"The Other Language." *Wisconsin Review* 24.2 (1989).
★"Martial Art" and ★"Variation on Death." *Jacaranda Review* 4.2 (1989).
"Nanking" accepted for *BYU Studies*.

ROB HOLLIS MILLER   P. 200

A native of Oregon and graduate of BYU, Miller has sailed as a merchant seaman and taught English in Saudi Arabia.
"Mormon Missionaries Bring Baseball to the Netherlands." *Sunstone* 7.2 (1982).
★"For Kathleen — marriage —." *Sunstone* 10.6 (1985).
"Sparta Butte Lookout." *Sunstone* 11.1 (1987).
★"Law of Gravity." *Oregon East.*
★"mythical bird" accepted for *Sunstone*.

KAREN MARGUERITE MOLONEY   P. 214

A native of Los Angeles, Moloney began college at Claremont as a Mormon convert. She transferred to BYU for a B.A. in English and drama and an M.L.S., taught in Australia and California, returned to BYU for an M.A., and recently finished a Ph.D. at UCLA.

*"Relinquishing." *Dialogue* 14.1 (1981). Revison printed in *Westwind* 29.2 (1986).

9 poems from the sequence "A Milesian Tel in Southern California." *BYU Studies* 23.4 (1983).

"Batiks." *Sunstone* 8.6 (1983).

"A Friesian Digging Southern California." *Sunstone* 10.6 (1985).

"Recollections from an Ex." *Dialogue* 20.2 (1987).

"A Bread-and-butter Note." *Sunstone* 12.1 (1988).

*"The Truant Officer Recalls Sweet Maggie." *The Jacaranda Review* 3.2 (1988). Winner, Elzer Poetry Award.

*"Snowfall on Glenflesk" printed as "Snowfall at Glenflesk." *Dialogue* 22.1 (1989).

*"The Viewing." *Sunstone* 13.2 (1989).

MARGARET RAMPTON MUNK   P. 138

Growing up in Salt Lake City, Munk attended the U. of Utah, where she began writing poems and essays, then moved to New England and Washington, D.C. Her one volume of poems was published in 1986, just before her death from cancer.

*"For Russ" and *"One Year." *So Far*. Potomac, MD: Greentree, 1986.

VENETA LEATHAM NIELSEN   P. 6

Nielsen taught English at Utah State U. for thirty-six years before retiring. She still teaches extension courses and leads a weekly poetry seminar. She is compiling a second volume of poems.

*"Nursery Rhyme," *"My Father Tamed Wild Horses," and *"Retirement: A Rhyme of the Sad Personal Pronouns." *Familiar As a Sparrow*. Provo: BYU Press, 1978. "My Father" reprinted in *A Believing People*.

LESLIE NORRIS   P. 273

Born in Merthyr Tydfil, a Welsh coal-mining town, Norris taught for twenty-four years at all levels of British education. Teaching brought him to the U. of Washington and, in 1980, to BYU for a writing workshop. He is now Professor of English and Poet in Residence at BYU.

Finding Gold. The Phoenix Living Poets Series. London: Chatto and Windus; Hogarth, 1967.

Ransoms. The Phoenix Living Poets Series. London: Chatto and Windus;

Hogarth, 1970. Alice Hunt Bartlett Prize from the British Poetry Society for *Ransoms*.

Mountains Polecats Pheasants, and Other Elegies. The Phoenix Living Poets Series. London: Chatto and Windus; Hogarth, c1974.

Sliding: Short Stories. New York: Scribner's, c1976. [Reprinted London: Dent, 1980.] "Waxwings," in this collection, won the Katherine Mansfield Memorial Medal in 1979.

Merlin & the Snake's Egg: Poems. Illustrated by Ted Lewin. New York: Viking, 1978.

Water Voices. The Phoenix Living Poets Series. London: Chatto and Windus; Hogarth, 1980. Won the Cholmondely Prize, the British Poetry Prize, 1981.

Walking the White Fields: Poems 1967–1980. Boston: Atlantic Monthly Press, c1980.

Norris's Ark. Illustrations by John Elwyn. Portsmouth, NH: Tidal Press, 1988.

The Girl from Cardigan: Sixteen Stories. Salt Lake City: Gibbs M. Smith, 1988. Won the Welsh Arts Council Prize for Fiction.

★"Christmas in Utah" and ★"The Dark Months." *Sequences*. Layton: Gibbs M. Smith, 1988.

The Hawk's Eye. Rexburg, ID: Honeybrook Press, 1988.

★"A Sea in the Desert." *The New Criterion* 6.8 (1988).

M. D. PALMER   P. 203

Palmer holds a B.A. in humanities and English and an M.A. in Humanities from BYU, as well as a Ph.D. in religious studies from the University of California at Santa Barbara. He started teaching at BYU-Hawaii in 1984 in communication and language arts.

"By the Rivers of Zion," "Revelation," and "The Searchlight." *Wye*, Spring 1972. "By the Rivers" reprinted in *22 Young Mormon Writers*.

"A Fugue on Suffering." *The New Era*, Dec. 1973.

"Still Life with Apples." *Kula Manu*, 1984.

"Damaris' Dream." *Kula Manu*, 1985.

★"First Spring" and "Reckoning: A Leaden Echo." *Kula Manu*, 1986.

"The Carpenter" and "Owl Haiku." *Kula Manu*, 1988.

"David's Music." *Sunstone* 13.1 (1989).

"Nude Beach Picnic" accepted for *Spirit*.

DIXIE LEE PARTRIDGE   P. 146

Raised on a small farm near Afton, Wyoming, Partridge offers a strong sense of place, history, and family. Her poems glow with a farmer's wary love of nature and an economy honed by years of study and writing.

"The Call." *Sunstone* 5.6 (1980).

"One Winter." *Sunstone* 6.4 (1981).

"The Burlap Years." *Sunstone* 8.3 (1983).

★"Deer in the Haystacks," ★"Wilderness," ★"Snowy Owl," and ★"Quickening." *Deer in the Haystacks.* Boise, ID: Ahsahta, 1984.
"Taking a Side Road Home" and "Dry Creek Farmer." *The Greensboro Review* 36 (Summer 1984).
"Farmer: Detail of an Oil on Canvas by A. Bertram." *Ensign*, March 1985.
"Angles." *Sunstone* 10.6 (1985).
★"Winter Horses." *Literature and Belief* 5.
"Release: Greeting Jade, Back from the Indonesian Mission." *Sunstone* 10.10 (1986).
"Absence." *Stone Country*, Fall–Winter 1986–87.
"What Changes." *Centennial Review* 31.3 (1987).
"Luggage," "On Seeing Part of a Cast-Iron Stove . . . ," and "Nocturne, October." *Dialogue* 20.4 (1987).
"Night of the Freezing Rain." *Christian Science Monitor*, 13 Nov. 1987.
"Light." *Ensign*, July 1988.
"Her Listening." *Commonweal* 115.17 (1988).
"Watermarks." *Commonweal* 116.4 (1989).
"Cliff Dwellings" and "Abandoned Farmyard, November." *Dialogue* 22.3 (1989).

CAROL LYNN PEARSON   P. 134

Born in Salt Lake City and raised in Provo, Pearson earned a B.A. and M.A. from BYU in theater. In addition to her poems, she has written nine plays and musicals, three novels, and four other books, including *Goodbye, I Love You.*
★"Guilt." *Beginnings.* Provo: Trilogy Arts, c1967. Reprinted in *A Believing People.*
The Search. Provo: Trilogy Arts, c1970.
★"Millie's Mother's Red Dress." *The Growing Season.* Salt Lake: Bookcraft, 1976. Reprinted in *Structure and Meaning: An Introduction to Literature.* Eds. Anthony Dubé, et al. Boston: Houghton Mifflin, 1976.
★"To the Sound of the Rain." *I Can't Stop Smiling.* Walnut Creek, CA: Littlefield, 1984.
A Widening View. Salt Lake City: Bookcraft, c1983.
Beginnings. 2d enlarged ed. Salt Lake City: Bookcraft, 1985. [Selections from *Beginnings* and *The Search*].

VERNICE WINEERA PERE   P. 115

Born to a Maori father and an English mother, Pere lived first-hand the cultural collision now shaping Hawaii, where she lives and works. As senior vice president of the Polynesian Cultural Center, she is helping to preserve some part of the island culture in her own poems.
Mahanga: Pacific Poems. Laie, HA: The Institute for Polynesian Studies, BYU–Hawaii, 1978.

★"Heritage." *Exponent II* 8.3 (1982).
★"At the Wall." *Literature and Belief* 1.
★"On Utah Lake." *Literature and Belief* 4. A Winner in the Christian Values
Writing Contest.

ROBERT A. REES   P. 96

As editor of *Dialogue* (1971–76), Rees has encouraged Mormon poetry with careful enthusiasm. He is currently director of the Department of Arts, Extension Division, and assistant dean of the College of Fine Arts, UCLA.
★"Somewhere Near Palmyra." *Dialogue* 13.3 (1980).
★"Gilead." *Sunstone* 6.1 (1981). AML prize.
"In St. Paul's Cathedral." *BYU Studies* 22.1 (1982).
"The Dancing Beggar of London." *BYU Studies* 23.4 (1983).
★"Fishers." *Dialogue* 17.2 (1984).
"Once at La Jolla." *Sunstone* 10.1 (1985).

KARL C. SANDBERG   P. 70

Sandberg was raised in the country of his poems, which are extracted from a larger work in progress, *Open Country* (formerly *Requiem for a Town*). He is DeWitt Wallace Professor of French and Humanities at MacAlester College and has been twice a fellow at the Camargo Foundation in Cassis, France.
★"Scripture Lesson." *Dialogue* 6.3–4 (1971).
★"Night Watch." *The Carleton Miscellany* 12.2 (1972).
"The Truth, They Said Anciently . . ." *Sunstone* 3.3 (1978).
"The Last Speaker Will Give the Interpretation of Tongues." *Sunstone* 11.1 (1987).
★"Autumn." *Sunstone* 11.5 (1987).

JOHN W. SCHOUTEN   P. 225

Raised in northern Oregon and in Provo, Schouten studied English and Spanish at the the U. of Utah, Latin American studies at BYU, and marketing and consumer behavior at the U. of Utah. In 1987 he moved with his wife and three sons to Ames, Iowa, where he teaches English at Iowa State.
★"Rain Coming." *Inscape* 2.2 (1983).
★"Night Walk." *Sunstone* 10.4 (1985).
"My Father." *Sunstone* 10.6 (1985).
★"Coming Home in the Evening." *Sunstone* 11.1 (1987).
★"Early Morning in Mapleton, Utah." *Sunstone* 11.5 (1987).

LORETTA RANDALL SHARP   P. 103

With B.A. and M.A. degrees from BYU, Sharp established the creative writing program at Interlochen Arts Academy. She has received Fulbright fellowships to India (1984) and Pakistan (1988), and a Klingenstein fellowship, Columbia University (1987–88).

★"October 9, 1846." *Poems of Praise.*
★"For Linda." *Dialogue* 14.4 (1981).
"Butte in the 50's." *The Red Wheelbarrow*, Fall 1983.
"Utah Valley Metaphors." *BYU Studies* 24.2 (1984).
"Breathings." *BYU Studies* 24.3 (1984).
"First Spring on Roosevelt Drive." *CutBank* 24 (1985).
"Poetics." *The Red Wheelbarrow*, Spring 1985.
"Wintering." *BYU Studies* 25.1 (1985).
"Sitting Desk," "The View of 12N," "Madelline," "Anne," "Stones," "Grandmother, Grandmother, Grandmother," and "Mother Ties." *Exponent II* 11.3 (1985).
"November 19, 1917—October 31, 1984." *The Red Wheelbarrow*, Fall 1985.
★"Walking Provo Canyon," "The Nature of Things," and "Poem Found on a Metal Bridge." *BYU Studies* 26.1 (1986).
"Language event." *The MacGuffin* 4.2 (1986). 2d prize, Poet Lore Competition.
"Judith." *The Burning World* 8 (Feb. 1987).
"Blood Poem," "Divestiture," "Julie," "The Table," and "Amelia." *Exponent II* 13.2 (1987).
★"At Utah Lake" [Published as "At the Lake's Edge"]. *Moving out* 13.1–2 (1987).
"Found Poem" and "Clarity." *X-Positive*, April 1987.
"Vision and Prayer" and "The Wash." *The MacGuffin* 4.3 (1987). "The Wash" won 1st prize, Poet Lore Competition.
"Bishop," ★"The Salutation," "Stones," "The Problem," and "Grandmother, Grandmother, Grandmother." *Dialogue* 20.3 (1987).
"Poem to Make David Smile" and "Poem for the Visiting Poet." *Contact II* 9.44–46 (1987).
★"Oleander" and "Billboard Women." *Asian Journal*, May 1988.
Twelve poems from "Handwork for the Lady of Tatters." *BYU Studies* 28.1 (1988).
"Accommodation." *Sunstone* 13.1 (1989).

LINDA SILLITOE   P. 185

A graduate of the U. of Utah and resident of Salt Lake City, Sillitoe has published a novel, *Sideways to the Sun*, and *Salamander: The Story of the Mormon Forgery Murders* (as principal author). *Windows on the Sea*, a collection of short stories, is forthcoming (from Signature Books).

"Trip Toward Prayer." *Dialogue* 6.3–4 (1971). Reprinted in *A Believing People.*
"These are the Severely Retarded," "The Reaping," and "Shivaree." *Dialogue* 7.3 (1972).
"The Buffalo and the Dentist." *Dialogue* 8.2 (1973).

"Still-life Study of an Ancestor." *Dialogue* 9.2 (1974). Reprinted in *22 Young Mormon Writers*.

"Waiting for Lightning." *Dialogue* 9.3 (1974).

"Rescuers." *Sunstone* 1.4 (1976).

★"Letter to a four-year-old Daughter." *BYU Studies* 16.2 (1976).

★"The old philosopher." *BYU Studies* 17.2 (1977). AML prize (1977).

"The Photograph." *Dialogue* 10.3 (1977).

"Approaching Christmas." *Sunstone* 3.1 (1977).

★"Some Nights." *Dialogue* 11.3 (1978).

"For the Artisans." *Sunstone* 4.2 (1979).

★"Song of Creation." *Dialogue* 12.4 (1979).

★"A Lullaby in the New Year." *Exponent II* 8.1 (1981). AML prize.

"the mine." *Exponent II* 8.2 (1982).

"oh how to be the wind." *Sunstone* 7.1 (1982).

★"Missing Persons." *Dialogue* 16.1 (1983).

"charm for a sick child" and "Another Birth." *Dialogue* 17.1 (1984).

"The Journalist." *Sunstone* 9.2 (1984).

"Sonnet for Spring." *Dialogue* 19.1 (1986).

"By the River." *Sunstone* 11.1 (1987).

"From the Laurel." *Dialogue* 20.1 (1987).

"beside the wheel." *Sunstone* 13.1 (1989).

"sonnet on life's dangers" and ★"During Recess." *Dialogue* 22.1 (1989).

★"Killer." *Sunstone* 13.2 (1989).

WILLIAM STAFFORD   P. 277

Stafford was raised among The Brethren, a group of pacifist Christians. His opposition to war and life in a Civilian Public Service work camp (1940–44) are chronicled in *Down in My Heart*.

Down in My Heart. Elgin, IL: Brethren Press, 1947.

West of Your City. Los Gatos, CA: Talisman, 1960.

Traveling Through the Dark. New York: Harper & Row, c1962.

The Rescued Year. New York: Harper & Row, c1966.

Allegiances. New York: Harper & Row, c1970.

Someday, Maybe. New York: Harper & Row, c1973.

★"Witness" and ★"The Farm on the Great Plains." *Stories That Could be True: New and Collected Poems*. New York: Harper & Row, c1977. [Includes the five preceding titles.]

Modern Poetry of Western America. Ed. with Clinton F. Larson. Provo: BYU Press, 1975.

Writing the Australian Crawl: Views on the Writer's Vocation. Ann Arbor: U. of Michigan Press, 1978.

A Glass Face in the Rain. New York: Harper & Row, c1982.

"Five Poems." *Sunstone* 8.1–2 (1983).

★"Scripture." *An Oregon Message*. New York: Harper & Row, c1987.
You and Some Other Characters. Rexburg, ID: Honeybrook Press, 1987.

HELEN CANDLAND STARK   P. 3

Born in Mt. Pleasant, Stark received her education at BYU. She has taught high school and university extension classes in Utah and Delaware.
★"Winds." *Improvement Era* 46.5 (1943).
★"An Early Frost." *Inward Light* 38 (1975–6).

MAY SWENSON   P. 280

Born in Logan and educated at Utah State, Swenson earned a B.S. and later, as a poet, an Honorary Doctor of Letters. She has published nine collections of verse, which have received many honors, including the Shelley Memorial Award of the Poetry Society of America and the Bollingen Prize in Poetry.
To Mix with Time: New & Selected Poems. New York: Scribners, 1963.
Poems to Solve. New York: Scribners, 1966.
More Poems to Solve. New York: Scribners, 1971. "The Beam" reprinted in *Dialogue* 4.3 (1969).
★"That the Soul May Wax Plump." *Atlantic*, June 1978.
★"Above Bear Lake." Reprinted by permission. From *New and Selected Things Taking Place*. Boston: Little, Brown, 1978.
In Other Words. New York: Knopf, 1987.
★"My Name was Called." Reprinted by permission; ©1988, May Swenson. Originally in *The New Yorker*, 13 June 1988.

ANITA TANNER   P. 169

Raised on a ranch in Star Valley, Wyoming, Tanner learned to love animals. Majoring in English at BYU, she learned to do the same for words. She currently lives in Cortez, Colorado.
"Divided." *Dialogue* 14.1 (Winter 1981).
"Scolding Bridle." *Sunstone* 8.3 (1983).
"Water Master." *Ensign*, March 1984.
"Awaiting the Thaw," "Morning at Mountain Meadow," and "Adam's Rib." *Utah Sings* 1985.
"Neighbor Versaw." *Christian Science Monitor*, 22 Aug. 1986.
"Evenings: His Church Calling" and "They Have Closed the Church My Father Helped Build." *Dialogue* 19.1 (Winter 1986).
"Awake at 3 a.m." *Christian Science Monitor*, 12 Jan. 1987.
"Coming In." *Christian Science Monitor*, 17 April 1987.
"Vision." *Christian Science Monitor*, 1 June 1987.
"Navel." *Dialogue* 21.3 (1988).

SALLY T. TAYLOR   P. 121

In addition to a book of poems and over forty-five poems published in various journals, anthologies, and collections, Taylor recently finished an English text-book to be published by Holt, Rinehart and Winston. At BYU, she teaches and oversees freshman English.

"Thou Hast Made my Mountain to Stand Strong." 1st place, Chair Competition, 1984 Eisteddfod, BYU.

★"Fading Family Portrait." *A Little Light at the Edge of Day*. Provo: Press Publishing, 1984.

"Jigsaw." *Gila Review*, Spring 1985.

"On the North Side of the Platte." *BYU Studies* 24.3 (1984).

"The Miracles That Didn't Come." *BYU Studies* 26.3 (1986).

"The End of Summer." *Cumberland Poetry Review* 7.1 (1987).

STEPHEN ORSON TAYLOR   P. 208

A graduate of BYU, Taylor currently practices law in Davis, California.

"A Psalm of Praise and Thanksgiving that the Universe is Not a Magnificent Mechanism" and "To Compose a Poem." *22 Young Mormon Writers*.

"To Compose a Poem." *Sunstone* 1.3 (1977).

"To MKT on His Birthday." *Sunstone* 2.2 (1977).

★"A Faun, on Reading Horace's Address to the Spring of Bandusia" and ★"Sophia." *Sunstone* 4.1 (1979).

★"The Love of Christ, and Spring." *Sunstone* 7.3 (1982).

★"On the Evening of President Smith's Leaving." *Sunstone* 11.1 (1987).

EMMA LOU THAYNE   P. 39; P. 264

Growing up in Salt Lake, Thayne earned a B.A. and M.A. at the U. of Utah, where she now teaches creative writing part time. Immersed in issues involving women, peace, and international understanding, she has published widely about those concerns.

Spaces in the Sage. Salt Lake City: Parliament Publishers, 1971.

Until Another Day for Butterflies. Salt Lake City: Parliament Publishers, 1973.

"Sunday School Picture," from this volume, reprinted in *A Believing People*.

On Slim Unaccountable Bones. Salt Lake City: Parliament Publishers, 1974.

Never Past the Gate. Layton: Peregrine Smith, 1975.

With Love, Mother. Salt Lake City: Deseret Book, 1975.

A Woman's Place. Salt Lake City: Nishan Grey, 1977.

The Family Bond. Salt Lake City: Nishan Grey, 1977.

★"Love Song at the End of Summer." *Exponent II* 5.4 (1979).

★"Massada" *Once in Israel*. Provo: BYU Press, 1980. AML prize, 1981.

★"Considering—The End." *How Much for the Earth: A Suite of Poems, About Time For Considering*. Midvale, c1983. AML prize, 1984.

★"Where Can I Turn for Peace?" *1985 Hymns*.
"Meditation on the Heavens." *Dialogue* 20.2 (1987).
"To My Visiting Teachers." *Ensign*, March 1988.
★"To a Daughter About to Become a Missionary." *As For Me and My House: Fifteen Meditations on Homemaking*. Salt Lake City: Bookcraft, 1989.

RICHARD TICE   P. 212

Tice works as an assistant editor at the *Ensign*. In 1985 he assumed the editing and publishing of *Dragonfly: East/West Haiku Journal*. He has translated or co-translated over 200 haiku.
"A Song of Celebration." *Sunstone* 1.3 (1976).
"Lanternlight." *Inscape*, Fall 1981.
★"Into Light." *Century II*, Winter 1981.
"after the wedding." *Frogpond* 6.2 (1983).
The Inside Track. Salt Lake City: Deseret Book, 1986.
Station Stop: A Collection of Haiku and Related Forms. Salt Lake City: Middlewood, 1986.
"The Significance of Snow." *Ensign*, Jan. 1985.
★"Decision." *Sunstone* 10.6 (1985).
"Church Historical Library." *Sunstone* 10.10 (1986).
"Bus Stop Snow." *Modern Haiku* 18.3 (Autumn 1987).
"the persimmon leaf." *Japan Air Lines English Haiku Contest, 1987–88*. San Francisco: J.A.L., 1988.
"Anticipation of the Shepherds." *A Celebration of Christmas*. Salt Lake City: Deseret Book, 1988

P. KAREN TODD   P. 219

Having earned a B.A. in communications and an M.A. in English at BYU, Todd taught English for a year full time at BYU. She now teaches part time and works as an editor.
"The Face of the Deep Before Dawn." *BYU Studies* 27.4 (1987).
★"Imprints." *BYU Studies* 28.2 (1988).
★"Christmas Present" and "In London on Sunday" accepted for *BYU Studies*.

PHILIP WHITE   P. 239

White is currently working on a Ph.D. in English at U. of Massachusetts at Amherst.
★"Seed." *BYU Studies* 27.4 (1987).
"Chronicles From the Street of Dreams." 2d place, Chair Competition, 1989 Eisteddfod, BYU.
"Three Poems for My Mother." *Dialogue* 22.2 (1989).

"Crabapples," "Flood," "Morning," and "After the Wedding." *Inscape* 1989, v. 1.

RONALD WILCOX   P. 86

Born in Holladay, Utah, and educated at BYU, Wilcox studied experimental theater at Baylor, receiving an M.A. As Residential Artist in the Professional Repertory Company of the Dallas Theater Center, he has acted in over sixty plays, written four, and published a novel, *The Rig.*

"Convictus, or The Navigator's Confession" and "Portrait of a Puritan." *Dialogue* 2.3 (1967).

"Prayers Public and Private." *Dialogue* 6.2 (1971).

★"Multiplicity." Parts 1–4 in *Dialogue* 7.3 (1972).

DAVID L. WRIGHT   P. 51

Born in Bennington, Idaho, Wright attended Utah State U., taught high school English, and served in the U.S. Air Force. He died of a heart attack in 1967. The first five titles below are stories.

"Speak Ye Tenderly of Kings." *Inland* 3 (Spring 1960).

"A Measure of Contentment." *The Humanist*, July–Aug. 1960.

"A Summer in the Country." *Mutiny* 3.3 (1960). Reprinted in *Best Articles and Stories*, March 1961. [Prose redaction of Wright's play *Still the Mountain Wind.*]

"The Hawk." *Arizona Quarterly* 16 (Winter 1960).

"Mice, Men and Principles." *Mutiny* 4.3–4 (1961–62).

★"The Conscience of the Village." *Dialogue* 5.2 (1970).

"Rich, The Dead Brother," "The Attic Boy," "The Owner of the Skull," "The Philosopher's Mother," and "A Gathering of Saints." *Dialogue* 5.3 (1970). "A Gathering of Saints" reprinted in *A Believing People.*

Jorgensen, Bruce W. "The Vocation of David Wright: An Essay in Analytic Biography." *Dialogue* 11.2 (1978).